Thank God
It's Friday

Thank God It's Friday

Encountering the Seven Last Words from the Cross

WILLIAM H. WILLIMON

Abingdon Press
Nashville

THANK GOD IT'S FRIDAY
ENCOUNTERING THE SEVEN LAST WORDS FROM THE CROSS

This book is printed on acid-free paper.

Library of Congress Cataloging-in-Publication Data

Willimon, William H.
    Thank God it's Friday : encountering the seven last words from the cross / William H.
Willimon.
        p. cm.
    ISBN 0-687-46490-0 (binding: pbk. : alk. paper)
    1. Jesus Christ—Seven last words. I. Title.

BT457.W55 2006
232.96'35—dc22
                                                                                          2006014903
ISBN-13: 978-0-687-46490-6

07 08 09 10 11 12 13 14 15—10 9 8 7 6 5 4 3 2
MANUFACTURED IN THE UNITED STATES OF AMERICA

Contents

Foreword
(or Forewarning)

A few weeks ago one thousand pastors and Christian schoolteachers eagerly awaited an uplifting word of hope from their first speaker. Instead, Will Willimon gave them a strong dose of reality, which, of course, was more hopeful ultimately. A fellow speaker for the conference, I listened with profound gratitude.

North Alabama United Methodist Conference Bishop Willimon, former dean of the chapel at Duke University and professor of ministry at the divinity school, is good at helping us look more seriously at the realities of life. Even more important, he is good at pointing us to the truth about God so that we can face life's struggles with a very hopeful realism.

In this book he does not disappoint us. He looks solemnly and urgently at the gravity of Jesus' last words from the cross and thereby reveals to us more of the depths of the heart of the triune God.

On the way, there are many surprises. Perhaps we have known the last words from the cross too well, so that they no longer shock us. We need someone like Willimon to remind us of the astonishment with which Jesus' cries and consolations and pleas can be heard if we aren't so numbed.

We are helped to face our own misunderstandings—and to comprehend the damage they do to our perceptions of God—by Willimon's own confessions of his confusions and errors. When he offers hard lessons for churches, he does so with wit and candor and thereby invites us into a shared shame and sorrow, repentance and restoration. He shows us the humor of our misperceptions and the irony of our reductions of God, even as he startles us with the horror of what Christ has suffered for us and quickens us with the intense faithfulness with which Jesus related not only to the Father and the Spirit but also to us sinners.

Beware! Willimon will not let us trivialize God—neither by our lives nor by our worship. If we hear these seven words truly, we will be too awed and shaken by the fleshly earthiness of the divinely emptied man, Jesus, by the supreme condescension of the sovereignly loving Father, and by the persistently upheaving winds of the Holy Spirit to let God be anything but God. We will not reduce the Trinity either to happy ditties or to merely dogmatic recitations. We will discover that the triune God loves us arduously, torturously, to the end beyond our wildest imaginings, and we will want to respond with humble reverence, passionate ardor, and steadfast commitment to honor the true God genuinely.

The daily lectionaries of several denominations in the church follow an order of praying the entire book of Psalms every seven weeks. In this pattern the Friday psalms always focus on repentance and sorrow and include Psalm 22. Following this habit for the last few years has caused me to ponder more deeply, especially on Fridays, that great Good Friday for which we constantly thank God.

In the same way, this book from Willimon will cause us to look afresh and more profoundly at the magnitude of what Jesus has done for us. The volume will be beneficial at any time but will especially require us to slow down and contemplate the weight of Holy Week with new gratefulness and a new desire to follow the way of Jesus in a willingness to suffer for the sake of the world.

Marva J. Dawn
Author of *The Sense of the Call: A Sabbath Way of Life for Those Who Serve God, the Church and the World*

*L*ord Jesus, we take a deep breath and prepare to stare at your bleeding body for three hours. The story, at least when told by Mel Gibson, seems so violent and sick. We don't come to church to be made sick but rather to celebrate our wellness. Church is the place for the uplifting thought and a spiritual boost.

What kind of God would make us come to church, and on a Friday too, and stare at such gore? Probably the sort of sick God who would love Americans, residents of one of the most violent cultures ever. All right, we admit it: we're birthed in blood, though the history books don't dwell upon it. We are the same people who rise up upon a mountain of bodies of slain Native Americans, lynched slaves, and enemies too numerous to mention, wipe our hands, raise our flag and proclaim, "Freedom is good." Talk about sick.

The NFL, the last Bruce Willis film, the hundreds of New Yorkers who murdered their fellow citizens this year, our children whom we are willing to sacrifice to further foreign policy, who are we kidding? We can't get enough of blood. Maybe you have trouble convincing the French of the necessity for blood atonement, but we Alabamians believe in the power of blood if nothing else. There's no way to tell the truth about us without having it as a story written in blood.

So we'll warn you right here at the beginning: any God who would dare to love us had better be willing to get his hands dirty. Any Father who would save us through his only begotten Son had better be willing to sacrifice his Son. Be forewarned: we can't tell the difference between our enemies and our saviors.

So come, Lord Jesus. Come on, spend a week confronting our government, mingling with the common people, parading in on the back of an ass on Sunday, partying with us on Thursday, getting mixed up with our legal system, and see what you get by Friday. Come and see what we'll do to you as we scorn your love, mock your reign, and give a gory reception to your blood-stained glory.

Come, Lord Jesus, and let's see what you'll do with us. Amen.

The First Word

"*Father, forgive them; for they know not what they do.*"
—Luke 23:32-38

Father, forgive. Jesus speaks the first word not to us but to God. For three years he has spoken to us, preached, taught, exhorted, instructed us. Now, as we have hung him up to die, Jesus, turning from us, speaks to his Father.

"Father, forgive."

Having been those who once were directly addressed, we are rendered into bystanders, overhearers of a conversation deep in the heart of the Trinity. Now, at the end, the once adoring crowds are gone; no one is left to listen to Jesus but the Father. And the word he speaks is a word that only God can dare say to God, for only God can forgive. We have no right to pray this prayer for Jesus. And what does the Son say to the Father? Of all the things he might pray, he prays, "Father, forgive. They know not what they do."

I've spent most of my life trying to figure out what I'm doing. Isn't that how they defined "human growth" in that child development class? "Human growth is the process of increasing self-awareness"?

We begin with naked instinct, mechanical reaction, hormonal response, but gradually, with puberty and a college education, gradually we learn where we are and what we're doing. We learn to seek pleasure and to avoid pain. We learn to avoid certain unproductive, dysfunctional behavior and to engage in more fruitful, beneficial conduct, and, now possessed with a keen sense of "self-awareness" we move reflectively, knowledgeably about the world, "our" world that, through our knowledge, we have made our own.

Yeah, right.

I took a course in seminary in Christian ethics. Christian ethics is the weighing of various ethical options and, through careful, rational deliberation, discerning the one right action and then pursuing that option in a prudential way.

Yeah, right.

I made an A in that course in rational ethical deliberation only to flunk when I tried actually to do that in life.

One little problem with our attempts to be thoughtful, prudent, reflective, and careful people: we're also the ones who on a Friday—just rationally following the best of Western jurisprudence—tortured to death the very Son of God.

Why? Well, we didn't know what we were doing. We did not then know, do not now know, will never know what we're doing. We're all stumbling in the dark. I once knew a man who, on sentry duty one dark night in France in the Second World War, was surprised to get a perfect shot of a German soldier coming toward him down a country road. When he went up to examine the body, he discovered it to be one of his best friends from another unit. He did not seem to be much consoled by my, "But you didn't know what you were doing."

Meeting with my stockbroker about my pension, I watched as he pulled out the charts and the graphs. I asked, "Does this mean that you have now elevated stockbrokerage from the level of casino gambling?" He said, "No, it means that I am giving you the illusion that I really know what I'm doing."

But we don't know what we're doing! It's a fact, not an excuse. Most of our malice is exercised without aforethought.

Roman soldiers, Jewish Sanhedrin, raving mob—how did each of you decide to murder God's Son? Well, we thought we were standing up for law and order. We believed we were supporting good biblical values. We were just soldiers obeying orders. We had this gut feeling. We weren't actually in charge of the proceedings; it was done by the government. Everything was done in accordance with the best legal advice.

In truth, it is as Jesus names it: "They don't know what they're doing." Wasn't that what the Tempter promised us back in the good garden? There was the Tree of Knowledge. Eat the fruit of that tree and our "eyes will be opened," we will know, that is, we will be just like God, for what is it that separates us from God? God knows everything, but we are severely limited in our knowledge.

At Satan's invitation, we took, we ate, and our eyes were opened. And what did we see? Our genitals! Our eyes were opened and we knew only one new thing: we are naked and afraid. Our new-fangled knowledge only exposed our vulnerability.

Matthew 25:31-46, parable of the great judgment, one of the nastiest little stories Jesus ever told. At the end, the Son of Man shall ascend the throne and judge all the *ethnoi*, all the peoples. On his left, the goats who, having not done good to the "least of these," having not recognized the incognito Christ among the poor, the imprisoned, and the oppressed are punished.

On the judge's right, the sheep—those who having reached out to the "least of these" are eternally rewarded.

3

Isn't it good to know the answers to the questions on the final exam? There will be judgment at the end, but on what basis? "I was in jail and you visited me!"

Here's the shock. In Jesus' story, the sheep talk exactly like the goats. Same words. Same reaction to the judgment of the Son of Man. "Lord, when did we see you?" The sheep and the goats talk the same.

Now, you expect the goats to be stupid. They didn't go to Sunday school, don't use gender-inclusive pronouns for God, don't volunteer for Habitat for Humanity.

But in Jesus' story, *the sheep are as dumb as the goats!* The sheep say the same thing as the goats: "Lord, when did we see you?"

The blessed sheep knew enough to visit the prisoner, give the cup of cold water, and so on, but they don't see Jesus any more clearly than the unethical, apathetic goats. They're all stupid! When it comes to seeing Jesus, in the end, you can't tell a sheep from a goat. Both have nothing more to say for themselves before the throne of judgment than the dumb: "Lord, when did we see you?"

Jesus' story of judgment is more than a peek at ethically correct behavior; it's a concluding symphony of ignorance. If you thought that Jesus waited for twenty-five chapters before finally, at the end, letting us sheep in on the inside scoop, forget it. The disciples who have had such difficulty figuring out Jesus for twenty-four chapters, in the end, are just as stupid as they were at the beginning. Following Jesus since chapter four, they go from dumb to even dumber by chapter twenty-five.

We're all amateurs, in regard to Jesus. There is no way to commandeer and to manage the sovereign judgments of a righteous God. Surely there is some way to be enough "in the know," to be politically progressive enough, to ensure that we are on the right side, that we can bypass God's judgment because we so knowledgeably see Jesus.

No. We don't know what we're doing.

This is a reach for you and for me. In the days after Hurricane Katrina, a much raised question was, How could a good God do such a thing? God's got some explaining to do for this one. In our theology, theodicy—the justification of the ways of God to humanity—is the only game in town. Trouble is, the Bible has no interest in theodicy, particularly in trying to explain natural disasters to humanity. Natural disasters are the preoccupation of biology rather than the Bible. In the Bible, it's more "homodicy"—justifying sinful humanity to God. It's human sin, not hurricanes, that is the Bible's big concern. Second Corinthians 5:19 doesn't say Christ was in the world, reconciling God to the world but rather God was in Christ, reconciling the world to God. How typical of us to think that it's God in the dock, God who has got to be justified to creative, compassionate folk like us. How typical, until we get to the cross.

And don't you find it curious that the first word, the very first word that Jesus speaks in agony on the cross, is "Father, forgive"? Such blood, violence, injustice, crushed bone, and ripped sinew, the hands nailed to the wood. With all the possible words of recrimination, condemnation, and accusation, the first thing Jesus says is, "Father, forgive." Earlier he commanded us to forgive our enemies and to pray for those who persecute us. We thought he meant that as a metaphor. (I can't tell you how long it's been since I've uttered a really good prayer for the soul of Saddam Hussein or Osama bin Laden.) On the cross, Jesus dares to pray for his worst enemies, the main foes of his good news, *us*.

How curious of Jesus to unite ignorance and forgiveness. I usually think of ignorance as the enemy of forgiveness. I say, "Forgiveness is fine—as long as the perpetrator first knows and then admits that what he did was wrong." First, sorrowful, knowledgeable repentance, then secondary, gracious forgiveness. Right?

Yet here, from the cross, is preemptive forgiveness. We begin with forgiveness. Jesus' first word is forgiveness. It's as if, when God the Father began creating the world, the first word was not "Let there be light" but rather "Let there be forgiveness." There will be no new world, no order out of chaos, no life from death, no new liaison between us and God without forgiveness first. Forgiveness is the first step, the bridge toward us that only God can build. The first word into our darkness is, "Father, forgive."

"Father, forgive," must always be the first word between us and God, because of our sin and because of God's eternal quest to have us. Forgiveness is what it costs God to be with people like us who, every time God reaches out to us in love, beat God away. Here on the cross, God the Father had two possibilities, the way I see it. One, God could abandon us. God could have said, "All right, that's enough. I did everything possible to reach toward them, embrace them, save them, bring them toward myself, but when they stooped to killing my Son, that's it." God could have abandoned us at this moment. Or, two, God the Father could have abandoned God the Son, handed him over into our sinful hands. God could have left the Son to hang there as the hapless, helpless victim of our evil.

But these were never real options for God if God were to continue to be the God who is revealed to us in Scripture. God the Father cannot be separated from God the Son. God the Father stays with the Son and in the suffering and horror gets us in the bargain. God the Father stays with us and gets a crucified Son. The unity of the Trinity is maintained—Father, Son, and Holy Spirit—and in so doing, the Father and the Holy Spirit take on the suffering of the Son. The Father of course could not have abandoned the Son without abandoning who the Father really is. So the Father maintains the life of the Trinity by uniting with us through massive forgiveness, for there is no way for God the

Father and God the Holy Spirit to be with God the Son, the Incarnate Word, without being with us murderers of God.

There, in forgiving from the cross, Jesus is only doing what he did throughout his ministry. And the Father, in receiving the plea for forgiveness of us by the Son, is only doing what the Father in the power and resourcefulness of the Holy Spirit constantly does—reach out to sinful humanity. The Son is doing on the cross what the Father and the Holy Spirit have done throughout the history of the world, only intensifying it, focusing it, through the cross.

This is why I said in the beginning that we are witnessing a conversation within the life of the Trinity. Remember the prayer of Jesus in Gethsemane? "Father, I don't want to die. Let this cup pass from me" (AP). Jesus was not playacting in that prayer. He did not eagerly seek the cross. And yet, because he was determined completely to love us and have us in the name of the Father, the cross found him, and he willingly took up the cross as the will of his Father. In how many instances in the Old Testament do we hear a similar debate as the Father says, "Israel, I have had it with you. I have tried to make covenant with you and sought earnestly to be your God, but now, with your idolatry and apostasy, I've had it with you. I'm out of here"? Then, just a few verses later, "Oh Ephraim, how can I leave you? How can I let you go?" And the Holy Spirit is so resourceful and relentless in getting intimate with us, yet also so elusive, evasive, free, and beyond our grasp, coming and going among us just when we least want the Holy Spirit to come or to go. Now, here on the cross, in the suffering of the Son, the Father is suffering what that Old Testament *hesed*, "steadfast love," finally comes to. And the relentlessly communal Holy Spirit is suffering the pain that intimacy with the human race inevitably entails for any God who would come so close to us.

Here on the cross, as Jesus prays, "Father, forgive them," we see that what Christ said in John's Gospel ("I and my Father are one") is true and that, because the Son and the Father are one, if the Son is to love and serve the Father and if the Father is to love and serve the Son, then both will take us in the bargain. And there is no taking murderers like us without a stunning act of divine forgiveness. The Trinity has reached out, drawn in, attached itself to us sinners, and look what it got—a cross. And we sinners have used every means at our disposal—including our religion, our spirituality, our faith—to resist this love, and look what it got us—forgiveness.

That's one of the things Jesus meant when he said, in John's Gospel, that there's no other way to the Father except through him. That is, there is just no way that we'll get to the Father except by the Father, Son, and Holy Spirit getting to us through trinitarian forgiveness.

I don't think it's "Father, forgive them because they are not really to be held culpable, for they don't rationally know what they are doing."

I think it's "Father, forgive them, for among other things, they don't know what they're doing." Of course, God will never get us except through forgiveness of our stupidity and cruelty. If God is going to wait until we *know* the wrong that we do, God will wait forever. If you are awaiting me to know, to admit, to confess my complicity, my sin, you will wait an eternity, and I am not eternal. Only God is that. If God's going to wait to talk with me until I first admit that I'm a sinner, the conversation will never occur. I'll be too defensive, too deceitful in my guilt. I'd rather die.

"Did you conspire to crucify the Son of God?"

"Who, me? Why are you always picking on me? I'm doing the best I can."

So the first thing we hear is, "You are forgiven." Then, "Can we talk?"

My friend, writer Reynolds Price, suffering from a tumor on the spine, in his illness, had a dream. In his dream, Reynolds was standing knee deep in the Jordan River, and there was Jesus, baptizing. Jesus looks at Reynolds and says, "My son, your sins are forgiven."

Reynolds snorts back at Jesus, "Who said I was worried about my sin? I want to be cured!" Jesus looks annoyed and says, "That too."

What an interesting progression here. First, "Father forgive," then second, "They don't know what they're doing." Thank God our relationship with God this day is not predicated on our awareness of what we're doing and who we are and what this all means and what were our motives. Our situation with God is determined by God. Preemptive forgiveness.

Reminds you of all those times when Jesus walked about Galilee on brighter days. He was forever walking up to folk and, without warning, saying to those whom he met, "your sins are forgiven," and "go, sin no more, your sins are forgiven." Almost nobody ever *asked* him to forgive them. Jesus knew that without forgiveness being the first word there would be no meeting of God and humanity.

There is that sense in which forgiveness precedes repentance. We lack the courage, the sense to confess, without the prior knowledge that our truthfulness and honesty about ourselves will not, by God, destroy us. So before there is truth-telling from the cross, there is forgiveness from the cross. Christians confess our sin not in order to receive forgiveness but rather because we are forgiven. Father forgive, they don't know.

When I taught preaching at a divinity school, I taught my students to be attentive to the very first words that they spoke in a sermon. "Your first words, the first couple of sentences, will set the tone for where you expect to go in the sermon." And the very first words that Jesus speaks are a prayer, "Father, forgive." What does that tell you about where this conversation from the cross is headed?

A few years ago, when great scholar of world religions, Huston Smith, visited Duke, he gave a lecture in which he characterized the most notable, most peculiar aspect of each religion—Islam, prayer; Judaism, family; Christianity? *Forgiveness.* It is distinctive of the faith of Jesus and to faith in Jesus to forgive enemies.

That this is the first word of Jesus is interestingly at odds with us. For us, if we forgive at all, it is a distinctly secondary word. First, "Let the offender ask for forgiveness, say that he is sorry, truly sorry, then comes forgiveness."

But at Calvary, nobody asked to be forgiven. Nobody said, "I'm sorry," or "Oops, I guess we're executing the wrong rabbi, forgive us."

And yet Jesus said first, "Father, forgive."

I believe that Catholic moral theology specifies that, in the dynamic of penitence in the church, for there to be forgiveness, there must be an "act of contrition."

There is none of that here. Only, "Father, forgive."

Is this Jesus at his most offensive, in his talk of preemptive forgiveness? Is this why we nailed him to the cross, in his forgiving us even before we asked and, what is more, asking us to forgive others? In a sermon on forgiveness, Augustine (Sermon 49.8) said that sometimes people in his church omitted the phrase from the Lord's Prayer that says, "and forgive us our debts as we forgive our debtors." Just passed right over that phrase silently because they knew it would be lying for them to say that aloud. They knew, says Augustine, that they were making a kind of covenant with God in this "forgive us our sins as we forgive the sins of others." In some of the earliest versions of Luke's Gospel, these words are omitted from the Lord's Prayer. Forgiveness is hard.

A rabbi once said to me that, while he admired most of what Jesus said and did, as a Jew, he found these first words from the cross among the most offensive, lamentable, and reprehensible. Why?

"We've had enough Jews crucified by gentiles. We don't need any more Jews forgiving gentiles for killing Jews."

I could see his point. When in my former congregation, a woman, being abused by her boyfriend, said to me, "I've prayed to God for the strength to be able to forgive him," I said to her, "No. First you tell him that he is wrong, that if he abuses you again, you are going to call the cops, have him thrown in jail, and then, and only then, if he stops, then we'll talk forgiveness."

With Jesus, on the cross, the sequence was different. First, he prayed to God to forgive. If we are meant to listen and to learn from the words of Jesus on the cross, this must be among the most distinctive, difficult lessons to learn, this first one.

"Who is this who forgives sin?" his critics asked. This day we, his would-be followers ask, "Who is this who *first* forgives sins— even before anybody has acknowledged the sin?"

Have you ever had the experience (I have) of having someone forgive you when you didn't ask for forgiveness? Maybe you didn't even know that you had done anything that needed forgiving.

In a conversation with a group of faculty, I said something about what a bad book had been written by a professor at another seminary. I added that I expected a bad book from someone who was such a jerk.

After most of the group had moved away, no doubt duly impressed by my candor and wit, a faculty colleague lingered and said, "The person whom you just trashed was the only person to stick by me in my divorce, the only person personally to offer me help and comfort. But I want you to know that I intend to forgive you for your boorish insensitivity. You are forgiven."

I can tell you, that offer of forgiveness did not feel that good to me. Until I got the forgiveness for being an insensitive boor, I did not know I was an insensitive boor.

Jesus' first word: Father, forgive. They don't know what they do.

Someone said to me, "My ex-husband has done everything he can to make my life miserable—before and after the divorce. I am so eaten up with anger and resentment that the doctor says it has affected my health. Can't sleep. Can't eat. I've tried everything. Now, there's nothing left for me to do but to forgive and forget him and hope to God that I'll be done with him forever and he'll forever be done with me."

Good strategy on her part, I thought. They say that sometimes you need to forgive in order to get the wrongdoer off your back, in order to breathe, in order finally to start over. But here, Jesus forgives, not in order to get away from us murderers but in order to get close to us, in order to save us. He asks forgiveness, not as a strategy for a more fulfilling life but because, as the Son of God, Jesus knows it to be the very nature of God to forgive.

Jesus first forgives. On the cross, before he asks anything for himself, he asks something for us: Father, forgive them.

Our culture first identifies the victim. When there is tragedy, we focus upon the victim. Stick with the victim, fix blame, assign guilt to the perpetrator after hearing the victim's side of the story. To move too quickly to talk of forgiveness appears to commit added violence against the victim and let the perpetrator too quickly off the hook. Yet Jesus, in his first word, focuses upon the perpetrators: us. "Father, forgive."

When a group of victims of sexual abuse by Catholic priests met with their bishop, and after hours of weeping, angry shouting at the sympathetic bishop, apologies, and offers of reparations by the bishop, when the bishop dared to mention the word *forgive*, he was shouted out of the room.

When there is injustice, wrong done, first get a lawyer and get even. Second—no, fourth or fifth—consider the possibility of exculpation, after there has been restitution and compensation.

Or we say, "The offender has first got to be made to see that what he has done is wrong, very wrong." Sin has got to be named, and claimed, owned as sin.

Yet, from the cross, Jesus forgives precisely because they/we *don't know* sin as sin. "Father forgive them. They do not know what they are doing."

Jesus doesn't just forgive; he preemptively forgives.

One day Jesus told a really inappropriate story about a farmer who had a fig tree (Luke 13:6-9). He came looking for fruit. For three years he's been looking for fruit. Fig trees are supposed to bear every year. But for three years, no fruit.

"Cut it down!" says the master. His servant pleads, "Master, let it alone. I'll put some dung on it, dig around it, then let's see what happens." The Greek, *aphetes*, can be translated as either "let it alone," or "forgive it."

"Cut it down!" That would be the just desserts for so bad a tree. However, "Master, forgive!" is how the story ends. Here, in this little parable of Jesus, up to our necks in dung, we are listening in on a conversation deep in the heart of the Trinity, a story that ends in forgiveness, as our story this day begins. There is thus, because of an infinitely forgiving and forbearing Master, still time.

Isaiah foresees a day when "the earth will be full of the knowledge of the LORD / as the waters cover the sea" (Isa. 11:9). Well, we aren't there yet. Today, this Friday, as Jesus hangs from the cross, as the blood and bile start to flow, we ponder the enormity of our cruelty and stupidity. This day, as Jesus speaks his first word from the cross, we first ponder the enormity of his grace. There is time. Father, forgive them. They do not know what they're doing.

*L*ord, you know us. We are big on justice. You have set in our insightful hearts a natural sense of right and wrong, good and bad and have placed in our powerful hands the means to make right and to do good. Give us some injustice, particularly if it can be televised, and we are off to the races, righting their wrong, teaching them a lesson they won't forget, using the gifts you have given us to make the world a better place, at least better than you made it for us, no offense intended. A just God demands justice-loving people. And we have learned well the lessons of history: weakness invites attack, a patient foreign policy only encourages tyrants, feed 'em today, fight 'em tomorrow, better to bomb in Baghdad than to have them one day knocking at the gates of Birmingham. The strong must look after the weak. The resourceful must protect the meek. We don't really mean to be eternally at war; still, if we want justice, we've got to work war, for that's our predominate, though extremely expensive, way of setting things right.

And if you, God Almighty, won't stand up and act like God, well, then we'll have to get organized and do it for you. It'll teach 'em a lesson.

So when they attacked us, we attacked them. Bomb Baghdad. That'll teach 'em. Evil for evil; it's all they understand. We'll teach them the joy of democracy, the preciousness of human life, the value of a free market, if we have to obliterate every grain of sand in their desert to do it. It'll teach 'em a lesson.

But then, when we had done our worst, you looked down from your bloody cross where we had nailed you and with your last breath worked your justice, saying, "Father forgive 'em. It'll teach 'em a lesson."

Your lessons are hard as nails. Amen.

The Second Word

"To-day shalt thou be with me in paradise."
—*Luke 23:39-43*

She was near the end of her life, her already long life. Now, in her late eighties, her body was growing weaker as she gradually succumbed to congestive heart failure.

I asked her, "What are your feelings now? Are you afraid? Regretful? What do you feel?"

And she answered, "No, not afraid."

"You have lived a long and good life," I said. "That must be a great consolation."

"Some. My main comfort," she replied, "is that soon I will get to be with Jesus."

That was her great comfort, as she came to the end. She would be with Jesus. Of course, it was a great comfort to her because, in a deep sense, she was already with Jesus. She had lived each day of her life, for as long as she could remember, with Jesus. For this woman, being with Jesus was not some purely future hope. It was a present reality. To be sure, one day before long, she hoped to be with her Lord in a fullness that she did not have now. But what she had now enabled her to look forward in confidence to what would come.

She was able to end her earthly life in such confidence because she had not waited to be with Jesus. Her whole life was a time of training for paradise. In a sense, she did not have to wait until she died to be with Jesus. She was in paradise with Jesus already.

Someday, one day, we will be with Jesus. That is the great hope of Easter faith. One day, the kingdom of God will shine forth in its fullness and we who heretofore have only seen through a mirror, dimly, shall see. One day everything will come into focus, and we shall see it all clearly, and what is promised today will be ours tomorrow.

That is one of the chief virtues of the future. Hope for the future keeps thrusting us out beyond today into tomorrow. No matter how lousy the present age, expectation of a bright future can keep us going in the difficult present. We may have it bad today, but tomorrow, someday, things will be put right. Eternal life begins the day after tomorrow.

That was always the way it was with Marxism, wasn't it? The Liberationist defenders of Marxism kept telling us that one day the great promise of a classless society would come to fulfillment. Marxism would be embodied in the true socialist state. But not today. The Soviet Union? No, Marxism means so much more than that sorry mistake. Cuba? No. Castro failed to get it right. China? No, they perverted Marxist ideals with their totalitarian state. The workers' paradise just never quite made it to today.

And that's the way tomorrow usually stands—as an ideal. If you keep it all future, a not-yet-attained ideal, then you never have to live it today, now. You can keep talking about pie-in-the-sky-by-and-by speculation and never need to embody your dreams here, take responsibility for reality now, today. When he called us ordinary people to "follow me," we didn't know at the time that meant all the way to a cross. When he said, "The kingdom of God is among you," we thought he meant that in the exclusively future tense (Luke 17:20).

Having spoken to his heavenly father, "Father, forgive them, they don't know what they are doing," Jesus now speaks to a criminal. He bypasses us and turns to the thief. He, who was forever instructing his followers, he who was always in prayer to his Father, now converses with a crook—in the disarmingly present tense. Now He, who got into much trouble with us righteous ones because he dared to eat and drink with sinners, now talks and dies with sinners. As Jesus hung in agony upon the cross, there was no one beside him but a thief. Well, not so much a "thief" as probably a "troublemaker," a "rabble-rouser," perhaps an "insurrectionist," maybe more accurately, a "terrorist."

And the criminal said to him, "Jesus, remember me when you come into your kingdom." The wretched man was surely thinking of tomorrow. For there, today with Jesus on a cross and a howling mob in front of him, in horrible agony from the worst form of punishment ever devised by wicked humanity, mocked before the world, any "kingdom" promised by Jesus must be in some distant future.

Jesus surprised him. "Today you will be with me in Paradise" (Luke 23:43). *Today.* What was conceived only as future became present in this promise of Jesus. You might have expected Jesus to say, "Someday, after I'm gone, when God finally gets things together and sets things right, when this horrible miscarriage of justice has been rectified, then you will be with me in my promised kingdom. Just wait until tomorrow."

No, Jesus said, "today you will be with me in Paradise." What a promise to speak to such a person in such horrible hell of crucifixion. Today, paradise.

Now one could say, "today you will be with me in Paradise" because Jesus and the thief were about to die, so that very evening they would be in the paradise of the afterlife. Both Jesus and the thief were on their way to death and therefore on their way to whatever life happens after death. It sure didn't look like paradise from where they were hanging. But I don't think that gets at the shock of what Jesus says here.

I believe that if Jesus had been walking along some Galilean road in the bright sunshine, rather than hanging here on the cross before a darkening sky, and if Jesus and the thief had had many years of life on this earth still ahead of them, I believe that this conversation would have gone exactly the same way.

For when Jesus speaks of "Paradise," he is not talking so much of a place where they may go someday, as *a relationship that they entered today.*

How odd of Jesus to link a grand notion like "Paradise" with the horror that is his cross. You may not want a definition of "Paradise," but here it is: Paradise is *whenever, wherever you are with Jesus.* Now to be sure, we Christians expect that that relationship will be deeper, richer, and more full once we have passed beyond the frustrations and limitations of this present mortal life. But that does not mean that that relationship does not begin here, now. Our practice of the Christian faith is our preparation for paradise. No, to tell the truth, on the basis of this story of Jesus and the thief on the cross, the Christian faith is our participation, now, today in paradise. The eternal, complete relationship begins here, even if not in its fullness, now.

The dying thief did not begin to be with Jesus in paradise once he had drawn his last breath. That criminal began his paradise the moment he recognized that the one who hung next to him in agony and horrible humiliation on the cross was none other than his Lord, the master of his life, the sovereign of the kingdom of

God. Or maybe the thief did not yet know any of that about Jesus—his lordship, sovereignty, and messianic power. (Because, as we have said earlier, knowledge, knowing what we're doing, is far too much to expect of us who, as Jesus said, "don't know what they're doing.") All he said was, "Jesus, remember me, when you come into your kingdom." And it was enough.

When we say "eternal life," that's a synonym for "God." God doesn't have an existence; God simply *is*. God is pure existence, complete life. When we say "death," that's a synonym for nothing happening and is thus an antonym for God. So when we say "God," we mean life, eternal life, that state of being where something's always and forever happening because God is life.

Only God has eternal life. Nothing in us or in the world is eternal. Among us, all that lives dies. End of story. Therefore, if we are to have eternal life, then we must somehow hitch on to God's life. To participate in God's life is to have eternal life, to be welcomed by God into God's existence, to be subsumed into God's story. And only God can do that. And whenever God does that, then that is eternal life. Here. Now.

This brief dialogue with Jesus and the criminal on the cross holds out the promise that, even in the worst situations of this life, it is possible to be with Jesus, here, now. What situation in our lives could be worse than hanging on a cross? Our God is not the sort of God who sits on high, aloof from the struggle and pain of this life. Our God gets mixed up in the mess of this life here on earth, even to the point of going with us criminals to the cross. If we want to be with God, in paradise or anywhere else, then we can expect to be with him at the cross. With this God, it gets very, very dark, and then we open our eyes and see that God is there, beside us. With this God, things go from bad to worse, from worse to awful, and then there, next to us, is God hanging in there with us, on a cross.

We need not sit around trying to envision some fuzzy, ethereal future in which we will "be with Jesus." That can all begin now, graciously made available to us, here, now. "*Today* you will be with me in Paradise" is not some promise for a possibility in the distant future, but it is a promise of what Christ can be for us here and now. We shouldn't therefore speak of the "afterlife" but of "eternal life," that life which is life with the living God, here, now. Even in the last moments of his life, that moment when he saw Jesus for who he was, the thief experienced paradise. He shined, even in this dark hour, the dying thief, suffering the same agony as Jesus, shined, his light made brighter in the reflection of Christ's eternal light.

So can you. Pay attention to those dark moments when you are forced by your discipleship to hang on some cross, when you are going through times of humiliation and pain because you are hanging out with Jesus. There, then, Jesus says to you as he said to the thief, "today you will be with me in Paradise." Paradise not one day, some day. Paradise now.

The great Russian writer, Tolstoy, compares his conversion to that of the thief on the cross:

> Five years ago I came to believe in Christ's teaching, and my life suddenly changed; I ceased to desire what I had previously desired, and began to desire what I formerly did not want. What had previously seemed to me good seemed evil, and what had seemed evil seemed good. It happened to me as it happens to a man who goes out on some business and on the way suddenly decides that the business is unnecessary and returns home. All that was on his right is now on his left, and all that was on his left is now on his right; his former wish to get as far as possible from home has changed into a wish to be as near as possible to it. The direction of my life and my desires became different, and good and evil changed places. . . .

I, like that thief on the cross, have believed Christ's teaching and been saved. And this is no far-fetched comparison but the closest expression of the condition of spiritual despair and horror at the problem of life and death in which I lived formerly, and of the condition of peace and happiness in which I am now.

. . . I, like the thief, knew that I was unhappy and suffering. . . . I, like the thief to the cross, was nailed by some force to that life of suffering and evil. And as, after the meaningless sufferings and evils of life, the thief awaited the terrible darkness of death, so did I await the same thing.

In all this I was exactly like the thief, but the difference was that the thief was already dying, while I was still living. The thief might believe that his salvation lay there beyond the grave, but I could not be satisfied with that, because beside a life beyond the grave life still awaited me here. But I did not understand that life. It seemed to me terrible. And suddenly I heard the words of Christ and understood them, and life and death ceased to seem to me evil, and instead of despair I experienced happiness and the joy of life undisturbed by death.[1]

Wouldn't it have been more fitting for Jesus to have spoken his second word as a word of comfort or explanation to his disciples, those who loved him and had followed him to this end, rather than to this thief? After all, to have believed that Jesus is the Christ, the Anointed and Holy One of God, and now to see him whipped, bleeding in agony on a cross, it's a shock. Were our hopes in him ill-founded? Are the mocking soldiers and the screaming mob right in their scorn for this "savior" who now needs saving?

Of course, such a question is typical of us disciples. We keep having difficulty with Jesus' reach, particularly when its scope is beyond the bounds of the inner circle, the church, us. Let's be truthful now: few of us, his disciples, were close enough for him to address. We had made it very lonely up there, at the top of Calvary. Humiliated, naked, reviled by the world in the most public and degrading of tortures, Jesus had to talk to whomever was close at hand. His ministry, his sermons, and his actions had now cast him among the very worst of people, in the middle of two of the commonest of criminals. Family, friends, disciples were nowhere to be found when the going got rough and the beating began. Jesus was alone.

There was no one there to comfort him in his need. Peter, the "Rock" had disappeared. Nobody but this crook to counsel him, nobody to talk with but this terrorist.

"Lord, we will stand by you," said all of us at the table last night. But that was in the quiet comfort of the family. Out here, with a howling mob and the Romans at last taking action, we say nothing and Jesus hangs there alone—except for a thief.

Earlier, we had complained, "This man receives sinners and eats with them" (AP). Now we might as well grumble, "The Savior receives sinners and dies with them."

Did he not say, "where two or three are gathered in my name, I am there"? I always thought that he meant that about prayer or worship. If just two or three of us gather at church on Sunday, he'll be there. Never knew that he meant it about dying thieves gathered on Calvary. Now, this day, in his Second Word, I see his point: *Where two or three good-for-nothing criminals are hanging out, like hanging on a cross, I am there.*

This, says the theologian Karl Barth, was the very first church. Church, like paradise, is wherever Jesus is with two or three of us. And look where he is now: on a cross. And look who is with him: criminals. Here, with two or three gathered with Jesus, is as church as church ever gets.

We just couldn't get the point when we railed against him for his temerity in eating and drinking with sinners. "I've come to seek and to save the lost," he replied. It never occurred to us that the worst of the sinners are those of us who do not know our sin and the worst of the lost are those who do not know how lost we really are. Now, the one who ate and drank with sinners dies with sinners—some whose sin is in their crimes against humanity and some, like us in church, whose sin is in our crimes against a God who loves sinners. The Word Made Flesh is born among us, heals and teaches, preaches and works miracles, is betrayed, suffers, and dies and walks into the halls of paradise with one miserable, repentant thief as his only prize for all his work. And this he calls "Paradise."

I know a preacher who was preaching a series of sermons on the Gospel of Matthew. He got to the Sermon on the Mount and began his sermon by asking, "How many of you here today have had an abortion? Let's see the hands." No hands raised.

"Let me rephrase that," said the preacher. "How many of you have had an abortion *or* have been so angry with other persons that you wanted them dead? Jesus both condemns you equally and also forgives you equally." The hands went up, embarrassed that Jesus has difficulty, at least in Matthew 5, in telling the difference between church and crooks. This God seeks company with crooks, goes looking for friends in low places, descends all the way down to hell and calls that "Paradise." This Savior, who got into such trouble for talking with anybody, has his last conversation with a thief.

The good news: Jesus Christ promises criminals a place in paradise, today.

I stood with her on the cracking concrete steps of the little church. I looked upon a forlorn concrete block building with peeling paint and rotting siding. One could not say that this church had "seen its better days," for one doubted if it had ever had such days, even when its badly whitewashed walls were not peeling.

Thus my breath was almost taken when she said to me, "I love this church. It's simple, straightforward beauty. It is what it is."

"Er, what would you say that it is?" I asked in amazement at the gap between her perception and mine.

"Why, it's a little bit of heaven to those of us who, at various times, have met God here. We've come here year after year, when somebody we loved died, when somebody got born, when we didn't know which way or other to turn, and here God met us. There's people all over this part of the county that have been put closer to heaven, nearer to our Lord, by what they saw and felt at this little church."

It's rather remarkable, don't you think, the difference in my impression of this bedraggled, peeling, run-down and decrepit concrete block building and her "little bit of heaven"? What's at the root of the difference between her perception and mine? The main thing was I had never met the living God here and she had, and that makes all the difference between a building and the body of Christ, between a concrete block aesthetic disappointment and the very gate of heaven.

In case you are ever in that part of Alabama, you may want to look up that church and see it for yourself. If you do, just ask at the bend of the road for the way to Paradise Valley.

Note

1. Leo Tolstoy, "I, Like the Thief," from *A Confession and What I Believe* (trans. Aylmer Maude; London: Oxford University Press, 1921), 103-5.

*T*o tell the truth, Lord Jesus, we weren't that close to your cross when the soldiers nailed you to the wood and hoisted you up over Golgotha. But from where we were standing, at a safe distance, it looked to us like your arms were extended just about as far as they could go. It made us very uncomfortable to see your arms stretched out so very wide.

Yet you tended to do that, even before you got your cross. Seeing you hanging there, arms in such unnatural embrace, we recalled how troublesome was your reach throughout your ministry, a real pain. First the dirty, common fisherfolk whom you called to abandon their families and follow you, then the tax collectors, the whores, the lepers, the stumbling blind and crawling lame, cruel Roman soldiers, bleeding women, clergy, even corpses, all responding to your touch, all caught within your grasp. A Savior can't reach that far and not expect to be punished for it. And on Friday, God knows you paid dearly for your barrier-breaking, boundary-bursting reach.

You overreached.

How wide is your reach? See, even now, the nails through your hands cannot constrain you. You stoop, strain, bend, and grab, reaching down all the way to hell itself, determined to gather, to reap, to have all us sinners, dead or alive, no matter what the sin, all in your clutch, all in your embrace.

We gather here, at the foot of your cross as those who have been grabbed, got hold of, by a Lord whose reach knows no bounds. So this day, this fateful Friday, we warn those not yet reached—Hitler, Stalin, the woman sitting next to us today on the bus, the man who yesterday cut us off in traffic and grinned about it, the one who so wronged me that I hate him and wish he were not, the Palestinian who strapped the plastic explosive to herself and pulled the cord hoping to take some Jewish children with her—beware. Take it from us sinners: His reach is without bounds, His embrace wide, determined and irresistible. He will have you, if He has to die trying. Amen.

The Third Word

"Woman, behold thy son! . . . [Son], behold thy mother!"
—John 19:26-27

Family was always a problem for Jesus. "Family Values" was not his thing. As a baby, his paternity was in question, and his birth was an embarrassment for many. As a child, he had problems with parental authority. "You didn't know that I would be about my Daddy's business?" he impudently asked Joseph and Mary when they reprimanded him for making them mad with worry by hanging out at the temple and arguing theology (Luke 2:49). Poor Joe worried about his paternity. "Son, why have you treated us so?" his mother asked after their frantic search for Jesus. What did Mary and Joseph do to deserve a smart-mouthed teenager like Jesus?

And when he grew up, he and his mother were at a wedding party. When the wine gave out and Mary frantically entreated Jesus for help, he brushed her off with a "Woman, what does that have to do with you or me?" (John 2:4 AP). Not the right tone of voice to take with dear old Mom.

And when his ministry got started, he thought nothing of reaching into a family fishing business, and with a terse, "Follow me," demanding that these fishermen abandon their aging father in the boat and join him wandering about with his buddies (Matt. 4:19).

"I've come to turn father against son, mother against daughter," he threatened (Matt. 10:35 AP). And he did.

"Daddy just died," said a man to him one day. "I'll sign up with you after the funeral."

"Let the dead bury the dead," said Jesus, in love. "Follow me!" (Matt. 8:22 AP). This had to be the reason Norman Rockwell never painted Jesus.

I vividly remember a Parents Weekend on campus at Duke many years ago, when the preacher—having read the story of Jesus calling his disciples, having them leave their father in the boat and follow him—looked out at the assembled congregation of students and their parents and noted, with more than a touch of sadness, "Jesus broke the hearts of many a first-century family."

One day, when Jesus was attempting to teach a gaggle of strangers about the good news, one said to him, "Your mother and your brothers are outside asking for you" (AP). Jesus replied, "Who are my mother and my brothers?" (Mark 3:32-35). Jesus and his family were not the Brady Bunch type.

At Duke, in twenty years as chaplain to the students, I had maybe ten or twelve angry, anxious telephone calls from parents. Never did they say, "Help! I sent my child to the university and he got addicted to alcohol," or "Help! I sent my child to college and she became sexually promiscuous." No, the calls I got were, "Help! I sent my child to Duke and she became a religious fanatic." Religious fanatic defined as, "she's going on a two-year mission to Haiti with the Catholics."

Give these parents credit. They know enough about Jesus to know that he creates havoc in a family.

So on the cross, Jesus once again gets into it with his mother. "Woman, behold thy son," he says to her. Mary, look at the child you are losing, the son that you are giving over for the sins of the world. Maternal love is that love that loves in order to give away. In Mary's case, it was particularly so. When Jesus was born, old Simeon had predicted, "A sword will also pierce your heart." From the first, it was not easy to be the mother of the Son of God. And now, even from the cross, Jesus is busy ripping apart families and breaking the hearts of mothers. Because he was obedient to the will of God, because Jesus did not waver from his God-ordained mission, he is a great pain to his family. "Woman, behold thy son."

But this is not the only word. Jesus' Third Word is in two parts. Having addressed his mother, Jesus, looking at one of his disciples, John, also says, "Son, behold your mother." Jesus is surely saying more here than, "John, do me a favor and look after Mom when I'm gone." Jesus is saying, "Mother, I'm giving you a new son. Son, behold your new mother." Jesus, the one who so disrupted conventional families, is, on the cross, forming a new family.

Most of us would do anything for our families. In fact, when it comes down to it, most of us don't do anything hard or heroic for anyone except our families. For instance, most of us are not violent by nature, yet, when asked, "Would you kill in order to protect your family from harm?" we readily answer in the affirmative. Few among us feel much responsibility for anyone beyond the bounds of our kith and kin. We give to the Red Cross most generously when the victims look like our relatives. Jesus has a considerably larger mission.

In that day, in that part of the world, there were no social attachments as rigid or determinative as that of the family. Family origin determined your whole life, your complete identity, your entire future. So one of the most countercultural, revolutionary acts of Jesus was his sustained attack upon the family.

In a culture like our own, dominated by "family values," where we have nothing better to command our allegiance to than our own blood relatives, this is one of the good things the church does for many of us. In baptism, we are rescued from our family. Our families, as good as they are, are too narrow, too restricted. So in baptism we are adopted into a family large enough to make our lives more interesting.

"A new commandment I give to you that you love one another as I have loved you," he said elsewhere (John 13:34). Watch closely. Jesus is forming the first church, commanding us to live as if these foreigners were our relatives. Church is where we are thrown together with a bunch of strangers and are forced to call these people with whom we have no natural affinity, nothing in common, "brother," "sister."

So after this moment, never again could the world say *family* without Jesus' people thinking *church*.

On campus one evening, debating the future of fraternities and sororities at Duke, this student says, "One reason why I love my fraternity is that it has forced me to be with a group of guys, many of whom I don't like—guys of a different race and culture from my own—and call these losers 'brother.' That's made me a better person than if I had been forced to stay with my own kind."

"I've never thought of a frat as a church," I said.

That day when they came to Jesus saying, "Your mother and your brothers are looking for you," Jesus responded saying, "Whoever does the will of my Father, he is my brother." In other words, Jesus is naming and claiming a new family for himself, that family made up of disciples. Now anybody who attempts to follow Jesus is one of the Family.

From the cross, in his third word to us, Jesus disrupts the totalitarian influence of the family in order to free us and give us a new, bigger family. He detaches us from parents to give us a new parent. We are to call no one "father" but the "Father." Jesus saves us from that too narrow, constricted, and constrained family into which we're born in order to give us a new, expanded, and more catholic family.

To be sure, our families are means of grace to us, but how ironic that our families, which ought to be such blessings, are often such burdens. But isn't that always the way it is with our sin? We pervert the good gifts of God all the time, including our families.

As a pastor, I can tell you that most of the really tragic stuff that happens to us in life happens in our families. A friend of mine, a therapist, says that most of her practice involves helping people get over the damage that has been done to them in the family. So one thing the church does for us in baptism is to adopt us, to rescue us from the ravages of a society that asks too much from its families, that puts too much weight on family values, in order to place us in a new family that's over two thousand years old with millions upon millions of brothers and sisters, living and dead. The church gives us more important work to do in life than merely sacrifice and take and give from people who look exactly like us.

My last graduation weekend as a campus minister, I said to a woman who was a graduating senior, an active participant in campus ministry, "I want to meet your parents this weekend. Will they be at the baccalaureate?"

"I wouldn't advise that," she said. "My mother's really pissed at you."

"Me? Why on earth would your mother be mad at me?" I asked.

"She's undone that I'm thinking about going into work with the poor. I think she liked the old me that she once had better than the new me who's working with Jesus."

Ah yes, Jesus, once again up to his old family-disrupting, mama-maddening, family-forming tricks.

Is this cross-induced critique of family good news or bad? I preached one evening at a church youth conference saying some of the things I've said here. After my sermon, a number of the adults, who had probably sacrificed most of their lives for their marriages and families, did not like what I had to say.

However, a significant number of youth waited in line behind the adults to say things to me like, "This is great! I have decided that I'm not good enough to keep my mom and dad together. I didn't know that God had any other plans."

So Jesus says to his disciple that he is giving him a new "mother," and to Mary he gives a new "son." At the foot of the cross, we who thought we were so different because of race, gender, or clan for once stand together, chanting in unison, "Crucify him!" Our uniting of nations is not a pretty sight, for our uniting and communing is always our attempt to get rid of God. But from the cross, Jesus stares into this crowd of crucifiers and thrusts us together by Jesus' loving solidarity. We, who once cared only for those folk who have the same genetic endowment as us, now are made to care for those with whom we have nothing in common except Jesus. We keep having that experience of coming to call "sister" someone whom we first thought to be just another threatening stranger. It's one of the gracious, demanding by-products of standing at the foot of Jesus' cross. It's called "the body of Christ."

We—who so long for togetherness, community, true family— are brought together, not by our great loneliness, but by God's great love.

How do you like this "family" at the foot of the cross? A big-shot businessman in our town was indicted for looting his company of millions, bringing thousands of his employees to ruin. To prepare for his federal court appearance, he got "saved" and proclaimed to the world, through his publicity agent, that he had "found Jesus."

(Am I being too cynical here?)

Well, who should I see on TV a month later, hosting a "Christian talk show," than this weeping, allegedly penitent thief! There he was, before God and everybody, Bible in hand, pious and sweet as a lamb.

It was more than I could take. "The creep!" I exclaimed to my wife, Patsy. "Is there no limit to his hypocrisy? Can you believe this?"

She, passing through the den, mumbled to me, "It's unbelievable the sort of creeps Jesus is willing to forgive. Even more incredible is the sort of creeps Jesus commands us to be church with."

She spoke the truth. If you think the family that you were born into is a pain, consider the family that we've been adopted into because of Jesus! I've said it before, I'll say it again: one of the toughest challenges of Jesus isn't just Jesus, it's Jesus' closest friends. Never forget that a major justification for the crucifixion of Jesus was the creepy company he kept.

Flannery O'Connor lived for a time alone and unknown in New York. She said that going to church in such an impersonal setting had its advantages. Upon returning from Mass at the Church of the Ascension on West 107th Street, she said of her time in church: "Although you see several people you wish you knew, you see thousands you're glad you don't know."[1]

The other day at our church, a missionary took up a collection for the children of Haiti. We passed the plate, and the offering was counted. It wasn't enough, said the missionary. "I'm going to pass this plate one more time," she threatened, "and when I do, I want you to pray one more time that Jesus will help you to recognize the faces of your own children."

Look around you just now, at these losers who gather at the foot of the cross, people whom you hardly know, much less have much in common with. Pray to God for the grace to be able to see these strangers as your siblings. Pray to God that they'll be given the grace to see you as a close relative. All of the inadequacies and problems that you had growing up in your family are being healed. He who had no conventional family, he who sired no children, is busy forming the largest family the world has ever known.

Welcome home.

Note

1. Quoted in Paul Elie, *The Life You Save May Be Your Own* (New York: Farrar, Straus and Giroux, 2003), 178.

*R*eally now, Lord Jesus, is our sin so serious as to necessitate the sort of ugly drama we are forced to behold this day? Why should the noon sky turn toward midnight and the earth heave and the heavens be rent for our mere peccadilloes? To be sure, we've made our mistakes. Things didn't turn out as we intended. There were unforeseen complications, factors beyond our control. But we meant well. We didn't intend for anyone to get hurt. We're only human, and is that so wrong?

Really now, Lamb of God who takes away the sins of the world, we may not be the very best people who ever lived, but surely we are not the worst. Others have committed more serious wrong. Ought we to be held responsible for the ignorance of our grandparents? They, like we, were doing the best they could, within the parameters of their time and place. We've always been forced to work with limited information. There's always been a huge gap between our intentions and our results.

Please, Lord Jesus, die for someone else, someone whose sin is more spectacular, more deserving of such supreme sacrifice. We don't want the responsibility. Really, Lord, is our unrighteousness so very serious? Are we such sinners that you should need to die for us?

Really, if you look at the larger picture, our sin, at least my sin, is so inconsequential. You are making too big a deal out of such meager rebellion. We don't want your blood on our hands. We don't want our lives in any way to bear the burden of your death. Really. Amen.

The Fourth Word

"My God, my God, why hast thou forsaken me?"
—Matthew 27:45-49

My church doesn't do too well in the dark. There was a day when a Sunday evening service was required of every Methodist church everywhere. But then came Sunday evening television and *Bonanza,* and today it's rare to worship God in the dark. That's sad because Jesus did some of his best work at night. He walked on water and stilled the raging sea just before dawn, taught Nicodemus at night, celebrated his most famous meal on a Thursday evening, and rose from the dead "while it was still dark." It's true. Easter happened in the dark. By the time we got there with the women for the Easter sunrise service, Jesus had already been raised and had eluded our grasp, dancing in the dark already back to Galilee.

But my church doesn't do that well in the dark. "I'm at a happy church, unfortunately," said a woman in my hearing. A "happy church"?

"Yep," she explained. "Everything is so happy and upbeat. The preacher jumps up on stage at the beginning of the service, just grinning and giggling. Looks like he may be on some kind of drug, he's so unbearably, insufferably happy. Every other word from him is 'Awesome!' 'Wasn't that an awesome song?' 'Isn't our praise band just awesome!' All the music is upbeat and giddy. It's hell to be going through a tough time in your life and be forced to worship at a happy church."

She reminded me of my last visit to an incurably "happy church." After the service, as we were all just grinning and swinging our sunny way out into the parking lot, I had to ask the pastor, "Is there no one here today with cancer? No one whose marriage is failing?"

Like I said, my church doesn't do all that well in the dark.

What words, what terrible, frightening words, this middle, dark word from the cross: "My God, my God, why hast thou forsaken me?"

This is the word that sets all the other words from the cross in context. This is the word that holds together all the rest, the word that uncovers the scandal of the words. Dereliction, loss and abandonment, words of doubt, hardly the words that one expects from the Son of God, the Messiah, the Revelation of God to God the Father. The Fourth Word couldn't have been the first word. If it had been, I doubt we would have stayed for the other six. "My God, my God, why hast thou forsaken me?"

And yet curiously, these searing words are words of hope. In the course of my life—in times of darkness and despair, when it has been my turn to walk the valley, true, a valley not as dark as the one that Jesus walked on Good Friday, but still dark—I may have blurted out some anguished words to God, but nothing I have said is as accusing, as angry, or as anguished as this: "My God, my God, why hast thou forsaken me?"

To hear these words upon the lips of Jesus, to have these words here, is a great . . . comfort.

Of course you probably know that these words were not original with Jesus. They are a quote from Psalm 22. They are words that Jesus learned by heart, probably still as a child in Sabbath school. They are words that were to be paraphrased as simply, "God, where are you when I need you?" Jesus is doing what we often do when we are at the end. There, sophisticated thoughts wither and we are forced by life to reach down into the recesses of memory. All we can remember is something buried deep within us from childhood—the Lord's Prayer or the Twenty-third Psalm. That's one reason why the church must make its children memorize scripture. In those dark times when we are at the end of our rope and we can't think, and most of what we once remembered has fled us, we need something that we know "by heart," something that we can say without having to think about it. So Jesus repeats a prayer, a clinch-fisted prayer, that he learned as a child in Sabbath school, a psalm of lament. "My God, my God, why have you forsaken me? / Why are you so far from helping me, from the words of my groaning?" Curious, we teach our children the Twenty-third Psalm, not the Twenty-second.

Having spoken to us, Jesus turns in his last moments back to his Father and prays, and his prayer is a grown-up version of, "Now I lay me down to sleep. . . . If I die before I wake, I pray the Lord my soul to take."

Jesus, in this prayer, speaks about the location of his Father. Having been so intimate with the Father that he could say, "I and my Father are one," "If you see me, you see the Father," here at the end, in the darkness and dereliction, he speaks in distinction from his Father, at some distance. "God, where are you?" is this prayer. In the weeks after the tragedy of September 11, I think this was the primary question, behind many questions, that were put to believers: *where was God on September 11?*

When insidious criminals pointed those planes toward the great towers, and the two towers fell in an inferno of destruction and death, where was God? These are words that are used only *in extremis,* when we are at the end of our rope, when things fall apart, and it is very dark: "My God, my God, why hast thou forsaken me?"

My analysis was that the question, Where was God on September 11?—how could God allow something like this to happen, why didn't God do something to stop it, what does God intend to make of all of this—depended for an answer, in great part, on where *we* were on September 11.

Perhaps you saw the public TV documentary, "Faith and Doubt at Ground Zero." It was fascinating to watch various people try to theologize their way through such a catastrophic event. When they had to think about the horrors of September 11, most of them thought about God on September 11 on the basis of what they had thought before.

For those who thought that God was complete power who would never let anything really, really bad happen to us, there was disillusionment. Others—who thought of God as a vague, distant, and impersonal idea—thought vague, impersonal thoughts that gave them some sort of vague, impersonal, philosophical consolation.

But for those who had heard words like these, their thoughts were formed by the Fourth Word from the cross. Where was God on that fateful Tuesday in September? Where God had been on that fateful Friday in that April. Those who said that this was "the worst that had ever happened in the history of our country" were possibly right. It was really bad for the country that had previously thought of itself as all-powerful, all-secure, and all-innocent and justly beloved by the world to know that we were not. But the worst thing that happened in the history of the world was not on a Tuesday morning in Manhattan but on a Friday afternoon at Golgotha.

There we saw the complexity of the way that this God saves, the curious way this is God With Us. There, as the best person who ever lived hung on the cross in public, humiliating, mortal agony, God the Father did not save God the Son from the cross or rescue him from this agony.

Why? Apparently this God has a more complex notion of power than we have. This God, to achieve victories, does not use our weapons. This God does not share our sentimental definition of *love*. This God, in this Son of God, is not somehow preserved from life's horrors but is present there. This God is so great that God does not despise or reject words of deepest anguish from God's children. It must be a great God who can be prayed to with words as tough as these. Someone must have deep, great faith to be able to pray this honestly to God.

Most of my prayers are, "God give me this, God grant me that. God deliver me, preserve me, rescue, save me." Jesus did not ask the Father for deliverance but for presence. Jesus' nearly last prayer was, "God, where are you?"

The One who was so close to the Father that he could declare, "I and my Father are one," is now at some distance from the Father. The Father is righteous, holy, nonviolent, and creative and in no way could bless such injustice and bloody wrong as that which occurs on Golgotha with his presence. So the Father sends the Son; the Father, as the Son, wades into the horror; and the Son calls out to the Father from the depths of despair. We are in a trinitarian mystery too deep for words, too deep perhaps even for the verbal creativity of the Trinity, so the Son speaks to the Father, by the Spirit, through quotation of a psalm.

Truly Christian prayer is, at its best, the honest prayer, "God, preserve me from trying to get you to run the world on my terms.

Save me from trying to get my life to work out the way I want. Bend me to pray like Jesus, 'not my will, but thine, be done.'"

Are these searing words any way to talk to God? It's Jesus' way, as the One who is most intimate with the Father. It's a deep, dark conversation deep in the heart of the Trinity. So this Fourth Word is a sign not only of God's near presence with us, down and dirty in the worst of the human situation, but also of God's great distance from us. Before these terrible words of truth, we might have thought that God was somewhat like we would be if we were God—loving, compassionate, considerate, and caring, as well as all-powerful, a great detached, omnipotent bureaucrat who can set everything right if he will just get going with his godliness.

That attitude seemed to be at the heart of the questions we asked after the Christmastide tsunami a few years ago. "How could a good God allow such suffering and tragedy to happen?" Translated: if God were as caring, compassionate, and considerate (and also as omnipotent, controlling, and powerful) as I would be if *I* were God, then . . . I sure wouldn't allow any suffering, injustice, or tragedy to occur on my watch—if I were God.

But in Jesus' words, in our listening in on the intimate talk within the heart of the Trinity, in this Fourth Word from the cross—God why have you abandoned me?—we discover that God is not like us at all. There is a vast difference between us and the Father. Our meager human analogies—God is like us: caring, compassionate, and considerate, only more so—just won't work when you are face-to-face with God on the cross. We think that being God means power, power to fix things, complete freedom to do what we damn well want to do, power to make the world work right, for our benefit.

Now, here in this prayer we discover God is at some distance from us, even at our most potent and compassionate. God is the suffering servant, the one condemned to die like a dog between two thieves, the one willing to be hung up and publicly humiliated, the one who is willing to send the Son, to give the Beloved into our sinful hands, in order to have us as we are. We ask Jesus to stand up and act like God and he just hangs there. So we see that what we call "God" is usually some form of Pontius Pilate power—force, power, shock and awe, violent means for a host of allegedly noble, but in reality selfish, ends. There is a sense that we made war on Iraq and we gave so generously to the victims of Hurricane Katrina for the same reasons: we so want to fix the things that God has not. The worst we do and the best we do are done for much the same reasons. As Aristotle noted long ago, we only make war in order to have peace.

But now, midway through Friday, look. The One whom Jesus calls "Father" is not in heaven, sitting on a throne, preparing to swoop down sometime and fix everything. The Father is there with the Son, hanging on a cross, now in intimate conversation with the Son, therefore not as the Son. We don't want to over-hear such terrible, terrifying words, "My God, why have you abandoned me," because we don't want to know that that's the kind of God we've got, the kind of God who does not always work the world to our benefit, the kind of God who, when it gets dark, doesn't immediately switch on the lights but rather comes and hangs out with us, on the cross, in the dark, and lets us in on the most intimate of conversations within the very heart of the Trinity.

The Father is one with the Son, in the power of the Holy Spirit. Yet the Father, in infinite love, has sent the Son out to the far country to us sinners. Away from the Father in order to be close to those who have abandoned the Father, the Son risks separation from the Father, risks not only abandonment but also dismemberment from his true identity. The Son comes very close to us, so close that he bears our sinfulness, bears the brunt of our viciousness. And the Father, who is complete righteousness and holiness, cannot embrace the sin that the Son so recklessly, lovingly bears, so the Father must abandon the Son on the cross because the Father is both love and righteousness. Here, in this word from the cross, is the unthinkable: a separation, because of love, in the heart of the fully loving, inseparable Trinity. In this world, love is the cause of some of life's greatest tragedies, and we know that there is no way completely to love anyone without the risk of pain because of that love. Sure, it's an inadequate human analogy, but we grope in our talk of such a mystery. What a sacrifice the Father is making in the Son's sacrifice, in the sacrificial power of the Spirit. There is a real division in the heart of the Trinity at this moment on the cross, and because the Trinity is inherently indivisible, the magnitude of the sacrifice is massive. The division that is part of the pain that must be borne by a God who would come out, in both righteousness and love, to save us.

Thus we can understand why, at first, Jesus' crucifixion was a problem for his followers. Some scholars believe that the very earliest proclamation of the gospel attributed no saving significance to Jesus' execution. For instance, when Peter proclaims the gospel in Acts 2:23-24, crucifixion is a tragedy that is overcome by resurrection: "this man . . . you crucified. . . . But God raised him up." A little later, Ignatius of Antioch had to launch an argument against the Docetists who taught that, on the cross, Jesus only seemed to die, only appeared to suffer (Greek: *doceo*, to seem). How could a truly suffering, crucified messiah be *the* Messiah? "Let the Messiah, the King of Israel, come down from the cross now, so that we may see and believe," we shouted (Mark 15:32). It took us a while to realize that by not coming down off the cross in glory, Jesus thereby proved that he really is the Savior who gloriously gives everything and risks all to seek and to save the lost. Only the God who loved Israel, and time and again risked and suffered for Israel, would be caught dead on a cross. Down through the centuries the church has struggled to explain just *how* we could be saved, justified, brought near to and set right with God through the cross. Theories of the Atonement are complex and only rarely helpful.

But today is not the day for theorizing about *how* we are saved by Jesus on the cross. In the Service of the Seven Words, the church does not include Pauline musings on the theological significance of the cross. It mainly just tells the story. Today is a day simply for sitting here and beholding our salvation on the cross. We are to adore, to behold, to gaze upon God's victory, experiencing it rather than understanding it.

So, what if the God Who Is is the God who in a stunningly bloody redefinition of love, "did not exploit his godliness but emptied himself, becoming a slave; he humbled himself and became obedient even to death, even to death on a cross" (Phil. 2:6-8 AP)? We wanted him to do something good for us, something great, and he just hangs there, impotent, mocked by the world, naked, exposed, now crying out in agony to the God who was supposed to save, saving by not saving, delivering by not delivering, embracing through forsaking, coming close by being so very different, true power in complete weakness, quoting a childlike prayer that everyone already knew.

Listen in on Jesus' prayer, his nearly final prayer, and you can learn a great deal about an incredibly odd God.

Back in a sunnier time, back in Galilee, on a warm summer's day, his disciples asked Jesus, "Lord, teach us to pray, like John taught his disciples." And in response, Jesus taught them a prayer: "Our father, who art in heaven . . ."

Here, at the end, in the gathering dark, he teaches us another prayer: "Our father, who art in hell . . ."

*T*he thing is, Lord, we only came along with the crowd because we thought the whole drama might be inspiring. We trudged up the hill because we thought it might lead to a real mountaintop experience. We had been feeling a bit blue lately, somewhat down, and could use a lift. We thought it might give us a renewed sense of meaning and purpose in life. And after all, isn't that really what religion is all about?

Frankly, if we had known what we know now—what with the gnashing of teeth, and the broken bone, and gushing blood, the screaming and all—we would have probably just stayed home and watched something on the Faith and Values Channel.

The thing is, it's hard to see what good this is going to do us or how this is going to help us feel a deeper sense of responsibility for the world or greater love for the human race or even a positive sense of self-worth.

We're beginning to wonder just how we'll be able to use any of this in our daily lives. We've got enough problems as it is without you making us stare at further unpleasantness. Frankly, some of this is difficult to understand, and isn't that the point of a sermon, to make You easier to understand? Amen.

The Fifth Word

"I thirst."
—John 19:28-29

When I was a kid, John Tarbox, the giant of a man who ran Tarbox's Drugstore, lived in a little house next to the drugstore. John came home early one Saturday and caught Sara Tarbox in bed with another man. Upon making this discovery, big John went right into his bathroom, they said, took out his straight razor and slit his throat, collapsing in his front yard. Sara ran out screaming, wearing her red kimono, and held him in her arms as he died. Later, when asked, she said his last words were, "I am so thirsty."

I both feared and respected John Tarbox, the one who gave us boys such a rough time when we came in to buy snow cones in the summer. Hearing of his bloody demise, I was most impressed by his last words: I am so thirsty. Hard for me, as a kid, to imagine that great hulk of a man, thirsting to death.

How can it be that the Son of God, the Second Person of the Trinity, would be thirsty? In the previous words from the cross, we have been theological. Now, as Jesus suffocates and bleeds to death, things get physical. "I'm thirsty."

The fifth word from the cross is a curiously carnal, bodily, somatic, and mundane word, "I thirst." It was a more appropriate word for Thursday, when, at a summit of Holy Week, we gathered with Jesus at a table and performed the most carnal of functions: eating and drinking. When it came time for him to do the last of his lectures, the sermonic summation, the point of it all, Jesus carnally said, "Have some bread. Take some wine."

How like Jesus, the Word Made Flesh, the Incarnation of God, to mix the fleshly with the spiritual, the earthly with the heavenly. On the cross, we encounter one of the most horribly physical events in the sacramental Gospels. Someone may be able to think that Christianity is something "spiritual," ethereal, floating off into never-never land, that is, until we gaze upon this wretched body, nails through sinew and flesh, heaving in final agony, in sweat and blood upon a cross, because of us.

Hanging on the cross, Jesus first speaks to his Father about forgiveness, then quotes from the Twenty-second Psalm, and affectionately addresses his mother as well as the thief, but now, he states mere bodily, personal need. This is his first self-referential remark. "I thirst."

As a preacher, sometimes I have been surprised by bodily need intruding itself into otherwise divine proceedings.

I remember a three-hour service of the Seven Last Words in which I preached. Though the host pastor had warned me, I got into the service inadequately prepared. My sermons were prepared, my ideas, but not my flesh. That meant that about 1:30 or a quarter of two, after sitting there for nearly two hours in that service, when I finally stood up to preach on the word, "I Thirst," I was tempted to say, "I thirst. No, really, would someone fetch me a glass of water? I thirst."

I recall preaching in a predominately African American congregation, where the service started at 11:00 a.m., but due to multiple anthems by the choir, a couple of different offerings, and ruminations by the host pastor, I did not stand up to preach until sometime after 1:00 p.m. There, my problem was not thirst, but after three cups of coffee before the service . . . well, anyway, there is something about us, as we are going about our so spiritual endeavors, that genuinely surprises us to find that we are, despite our noble intellectual or spiritual virtues, *creatures.*

And with Jesus, there is something about us creatures that wants to make Jesus God *uncarnate.* Here is Jesus—a great spiritual leader, a marvelous teacher of high wisdom, a purveyor of some of the most noble notions ever uttered. That way we can keep him high and lifted up, floating somewhere above the grubby particularities of life. He can mean as much to us as Plato. He can be exclusively *spiritual* and therefore irrelevant.

But not now. After speaking words to God, Jesus speaks of himself. "I thirst." Against all Docetic tendencies, these words force us to reckon with the reality that Jesus is in the flesh. His suffering is real. The drops of blood, the sweat, the torn flesh. Real.

On campus, "Don't you think it's wonderful that there is so much interest these days in spirituality?"

"Wouldn't know about that, certainly wouldn't be excited about that. I'm a Christian. We're not spiritual. We're into the physical. Can you say *incarnation?*"

I remember a particularly excruciating (no pun intended) sermon (and at a wedding of all places) by a Baptist preacher who appeared to feel that every sermon, no matter from what text or on what occasion, ought to recite the entire history of salvation, from Genesis to Revelation, culminating in Jesus' sacrificial, atoning death upon the cross. His sermon was mostly consumed with graphic descriptions of how horrible a crucifixion would be. The congregation, whom I could see from where I was sitting, appeared to be turning slightly nauseated as he described nails going through hands. "Have you ever thought of a nail being driven into the middle of a human hand?" he roared. The spear going into the side, with the blood and the water gushing forth. The crown of thorns, the whipping alone, from which many people died, all of that done to Jesus.

It all seemed to me graphically, physically excessive. Excruciating. But then, to give the preacher credit, I realized that he was dealing with people like us, spiritual people who have gone to extraordinary lengths to rise above our "in-carnality." We were at a wedding, after all, in which a couple was getting ready to do with their bodies that which they had felt in their hearts, a wedding, where a couple comes to church as a prelude to coitus.

The Christian faith has got its hands full teaching people like us that, if we are going to meet God, we will meet God in the flesh. We live in air-conditioned homes. At any given moment, millions of us are on medication that dulls our experience of bodily pain and presence. I get a pain, I pop a pill, and I can go right on deluding myself about my essential carnality.

I've got a friend who refuses to watch nature programs on television, even National Geographic specials on the survival of hippopotami. He calls them, "Nature Exploitation Shows." He thinks that it is morally debilitating for us to watch a tiger hunting down and killing a zebra, or a crocodile devouring a water buffalo. He is unmoved when I say, "Well, that is nature. Tooth, claw, and nail nature." He thinks that, as modern people, we have seen so many millions of images of this sort of "natural" violence and bloodletting that we have become immune. Now there is nothing within us that is moved by jaws crushing bone and ripping bloody flesh. It is just another evening of television.

His could be a good rationale for avoiding the evening news. After you have seen your thousandth child sitting in the rubble of her village in the West Bank, after, for the two-hundredth time, you have seen the screaming mother running through the streets of a town in Iraq holding her baby after our bomb hit her house, you begin not even to have a twitch of sympathy. You are numb.

In case we would try to do anything like that with the suffering of Jesus, he cries out with these words, "I thirst."

I think this is one reason the Gospels are so relatively terse in their descriptions of the crucifixion—none of the explicit, sentimental blood and gore of say Mel Gibson's *Passion*. They just report, "they did this," then "they did that," without more gory detail. Lots of room left for our imagination, little opportunity given for us to make too much out of our cruelty. Nothing now but the simple, "I thirst."

In Honduras, an esteemed surgeon, who was also a devout Catholic, one day in the clinic picked up a naked little boy, a child of no more than four or five, and asked me to touch the boy's bloated belly. With tears in his eyes, the surgeon said, "This little boy has no more than a month to live with malnutrition this advanced. His little, empty stomach is about the most obscene thing I've ever seen."

Only the sacramental worship of a God in the flesh could teach a modern Western person like him the obscenity of human starvation.

This Fifth Word is curious in light of Jesus' repeated statements that he was the ultimate thirst quencher. "Whoever believes in me will never be thirsty," was a claim that he made many times (John 4:14; 6:35). If you're thirsty, come to me, he said (John 7:37). The Thirst Quencher is now thirsty? This "I thirst" must mean more than simply that Jesus was, after all, not only divine but also human. In his saying, "I thirst," we may be at the very heart of his divinity, that which makes Jesus God, one with the Father, and so very much unlike us.

In the Bible, to "thirst" is usually for more than water. To thirst in Scripture is to yearn, to long for, to be desperate with desire. Jesus, in the beginning of his Sermon on the Mount, blessed a certain sort of holy desperation. "Blessed are those who hunger and thirst for righteousness" (Matt. 5:6). Blessed are those who want God's will to be done on earth as it is in heaven as if they were desperate for a drink of water after a week in the desert. The psalmist prays, "My soul thirsts for God, for the living God" (Ps. 42:2).

I am remembering, from my youth, a long and grueling hike up a dusty trail in the mountains on a desiccating, hot day. We had all taken water with us, as instructed, but a little over an hour into the hike, all of our water was gone. We had to keep walking for another hour or so. When we finally came upon a mountain creek, everyone burst into a gallop, and, reaching the creek, we threw ourselves into the creek, pushing and pulling one another out of the way, falling in face down, lapping up the water like the thirsty animals that we were.

In a Honduran village I watched brave women, trudging halfway up the steep mountain, day after day, with huge tin watering cans on their backs, desperate for life-giving water for their families.

When, in New Orleans after Katrina, civil unrest broke out, the General in charge said, "You keep potable water from people and they will destroy the city to get a drink."

Jesus blessed people who were that way about the righteousness of God. He blessed people who were eaten up with the desire to be with God, to see God's will done on earth as it is in heaven.

C. S. Lewis said that the trouble with many of us is not that we are bad, just that we are "too easily pleased." We are too satisfied with things as they are, too adjusted and accommodated to the status quo, not thirsty. For us, it is a sign of immaturity for a person to be too eager, too single-mindedly in pursuit of something. The mature learn to step back, to live with balance and cool discretion. Most of us long for balance in our lives, equilibrium and serene contentment. But that was the way of the Buddha, not Jesus. Jesus blessed those who thirsted after God like a thirsty animal.

Ever seen a person truly thirsty for righteousness? I was at a conference on justice and spirituality at Messiah College in Pennsylvania. We sat around for a couple of days, a group of scholars and students, discussing biblical concepts of justice, having historical lectures on the prophets of Israel and their meaning. Toward the end of the second day, in a panel discussion on "*Dikaiosune* in the Letters of Paul," this sophomore rose up from his seat and started shouting, "Do you people know what Israel is doing in the occupied territories? I've just come back from Ramallah. Here we sit, talking about justice and not one hand is lifted in concern, not one word about the suffering and injustice there!"

We informed the student that such outbursts were not appreciated in academic gatherings. We urged him to behave in a more rational manner, to see all sides of the issue without settling down on any of them, to step back, cool off, tone down, and act more intellectual.

He stormed out, just about to die for some justice, thirsty for a drink that only God could give.

"Our hearts are restless [i.e., thirsty] until they find rest in thee," said Augustine.

Here, at the cross, we are now not splashing about in the shallow end of the pool. Here, even the most complacent minds realize that Jesus has led us into deep waters. Here, religion is significantly more than something "spiritual," more than an uplifting thought or noble idea that we can all sit around and discuss and then go home and forget. Here religion has somehow taken hold of our whole being, consumed us, knocked us off balance, and demanded our last anguished breath. Jesus says, "I thirst."

There is a parched desiccation within us that will only be assuaged by God, by the living God. In his deep anguish, in his thirsting, they offered him a sponge with vinegar on a stick. But Jesus was thirsty for more than water. Jesus had a deep, blessed thirst that God's will be done on earth as in heaven, that God's righteousness might be fulfilled to the brim, a holy thirst that could only be assuaged, by lifting up the bloodred cup of salvation and drinking it to the dregs.

But maybe Jesus isn't talking about *our* thirst or *our* hunger. He says "I" thirst. Not you, not me. He said, "*I* thirst." God Almighty, the Son of the Father is thirsty. The mocking soldiers offered him a sponge soaked in vinegar just to scorn him in his thirst.

But maybe he wasn't thirsty even for water. Maybe he was thirsty for his righteousness' sake. Maybe he was thirsty for *us*. Is not that a fair summary of much of Scripture—God's got this thing for us? God is determined—through Creation, the words of the prophets, the teaching of the law, the birth of the Christ—to get close to us. God has this unquenchable thirst to have us. Even us.

Sorry, if you thought when we say "God" we have in mind some impersonal power, some fair-minded and balanced bureaucrat who is skilled at the careful administration of natural law from a safe distance in eternity. Our God is intensely, unreservedly personal. The God of Israel and the church refuses ever to be an abstraction or a generality. In the Bible, God gets angry, changes his mind, makes threats, promises, and punishes. Only persons do such things and, when we do them, it is a sign of our personal worth, not of our grubby anthropocentric imperfection.

That's one of the things we mean when we say that "Jesus is Lord," or "Jesus is God's only Son." We mean that this God is shockingly personal, available, present. And to say that is in no way a detraction from the Father's immense deity. There are gods who could not risk getting this close to us. We are killers who tend to kill our would-be saviors. Because we so want to be gods unto ourselves, we are rough on any who would presume to rule over us. So most "gods" are careful to keep their distance from us through abstraction and generalization.

This God, the one whom Israel and the church know as Trinity, is so great as to be able to be utterly personal, available, and present to us. This God is against balance and reserve. This God thirsts for us, wholeheartedly gives himself over to us, unabashedly gets close to us. You can't get much closer to us, to the real us, than a cross.

When Christians say that God is transcendent or distant, this is what we are trying to say. The hiddenness of God is precisely in God's nearby self-revelation as God on the cross. It's God's difference from our expectations for gods that makes God hidden to us. We are blinded to God on the cross by our assumption that if there were a true God, that God would be somewhere a long way from us, not here before us, naked, exposed, and on a cross. I'm saying that Jesus' "I thirst" is another way of revealing God's utter self-giving availability to us.

So, in Psalm Twenty-three, when the psalmist says, in most of our translations, "Surely goodness and mercy shall follow me all the days of my life: and I will dwell in the house of the LORD for ever," I discovered that the Hebrew word translated most of the time as "follow" can also be rendered as "pursue." In fact, in a number of other places in the Old Testament, that's just how it is translated. "Our enemies pursued us."

That certainly colors God's goodness and mercy in a different way, doesn't it? It's one thing to have goodness and mercy tag along behind you all your days, but it's quite another to be stalked, tracked down, cornered by goodness and mercy pursuing you just when you thought that you were at last on your own. Here we are, all self-sufficient and liberated, only to climb up the mountain to find goodness and mercy ready to jump us from a bloody cross.

Despite our earnest efforts, we couldn't climb all the way up to God. So what did God do? In an amazing act of condescension, on Good Friday, God climbed down to us, became one with us. The story of divine condescension begins on Christmas and ends on Good Friday. We thought, if there is to be business between us and God, we must somehow get up to God. Then God came down, down to the level of the cross, all the way down to the depths of hell. He who knew not sin took on our sin so that we might be free of it. God still stoops, in your life and mine, condescends.

"Are you able to drink the cup that I am to drink?" he asked his disciples, before his way up Golgotha. Our answer is an obvious, "No!" His cup is not only the cup of crucifixion and death, it is the bloody, bloody cup that one must drink if one is going to get mixed up in us. Any God who would wander into the human condition, any God who has this thirst to pursue us, had better not be too put off by pain, for that's the way we tend to treat our saviors. Any God who tries to love us had better be ready to die for it.

As Chesterton writes, "Any man who preaches real love is bound to beget hate . . . Real love has always ended in bloodshed."[1]

Earlier in this very same gospel, it was said, "The Word, the eternal Logos of God, became flesh and moved in with us, and we beheld his glory" (AP). Now the Word, the Christ of God, sees where so reckless a move ends: on a cross. "I thirst, I yearn to feast with you," he says, "and behold, if you dare, where it gets me."

When I was giving some lectures at a seminary in Sweden some years ago, a seminarian asked, "Do you really think Jesus Christ is the only way for us to get to God?"

And I thoughtfully replied, "I'll just say this, if you were born in South Carolina, and living in George W. Bush's America, yes. There really is no way for somebody like me to get to God, other than a Savior who doesn't mind a little blood and gore, a bit of suffering and grizzly shock and awe, in order to get to me. A nice, balanced Savior couldn't do much for a guy like me. I need a fanatic like Jesus. For we have demonstrated that we are an awfully, fanatically cruel and bloody people when our security is threatened. We have this history of murdering our saviors. So I just can't imagine any other way to God except Jesus."

God's in this fix, on this day, because God's so thirsty for us.

Note

1. G. K. Chesterton, *Orthodoxy* (New York: Doubleday, 1990), 143.

*L*ord, here's what we need today, right away, or as soon as we can get it: we need world peace, prosperity, security, life without risk, pleasure without pain, happiness without cost, and discipleship with no cross. That's why we're here, at church, to get our needs met. Our church tries to be user-friendly and seeker sensitive. That's why on Sundays we serve espresso with a dash of amaretto before our services, a little caffeine boost until we get to the main point of our worship: the prayer requests. So like we were saying, we need a quick recovery from gall bladder surgery, an effortless cataract removal, a happy marriage, obedient and chaste kids, and a reason to get out of bed in the morning. If you love us, you'll meet our needs.

Now then, is there something that we could do for you?

You're thirsty? Well, if you're the Messiah, why don't you fix yourself a divine drink? We've got needs of our own, thank you. It's our job to have need; it's your job to meet need.

For this and all other needs, spoken and unspoken, felt and unfelt, incipient and obvious, personal and corporate, immediate and long term, we pray. Amen.

The Sixth Word

"It is finished."
—*John 19:30*

The Sixth Word is a word of completion and resolution. "It is finished." When Jesus says from the cross, "It is finished," it could be read as a word of desperate surrender, of final relenting capitulation. I give up. It could be read that way. And while it took most victims longer to die on a cross, Jesus has fought quite a battle in his hours hanging in agony. Perhaps these words show that he has finally relented and given in.

There can be virtue in surrender. I heard a stock market analyst say a while back that it took a courageous investor to sell a losing stock. Most investors, he said, would hold on to an habitually losing stock, rather than sell, because the pain of losing the money was much less than the pain of having to admit that you were dumb to buy that stock in the first place. Only the truly smart, truly courageous, and virtuous investor was able to know when to fold, when to surrender, when to say "I goofed." Is that what Jesus is doing here?

It was a good campaign while it lasted; he gave it his best shot. Perhaps if he had been a bit more critical in his selection of disciples, he might have gotten better disciples. If he had been a bit more conciliatory toward Pilate, perhaps this thing would have gone a bit further. Now, it is finished. The End.

But I am hearing this word, this Sixth Word before the final word, in a different way. I am hearing this word as a word of achievement and completion. I am hearing this word as the same word Michelangelo uttered when he put his last touch of paint on the ceiling of the Sistine Chapel. Jesus has fought the good fight, and, despite what the soldiers, the politicians, and the howling mob before him think, despite even what his own disciples think, he has succeeded. He has done it. He did not say, "I am finished." He said, "*It* is finished." His work is done. "He hath poured out his soul unto death: and he was numbered with the transgressors; and he bare the sin of many, and made intercession for the transgressors" (Isa. 53:12 KJV). Jesus didn't die as a frustrated failed revolutionary. His death was the revolution.

Years ago I did a book on burnout among clergy. I interviewed scores of clergy who had called it quits. One pastor said he found that one of the most debilitating aspects of parish ministry was that, "It's never finished." There is always one more sermon to be written, one more book to be read, one more hurting person to be visited and counseled.

"God, how I envy housepainters!" another ex-pastor said. "They can actually see the results of their work. They get done!" What a joy it is to have an ending, to be able to say that it is over and done with. That was one of the things I loved most about the academic life: commencement. No matter how bad the year had been, no matter how many disappointing students I had taught or lousy lectures I had delivered, there was always that day in May when *it was over*.

Today a work is being done, a work that Jesus did not at first enthusiastically undertake. He prayed in Gethsemane that this cup might pass. He did not want to die. And yet, when it became clear to him that this was indeed the Father's will, the Son who was one with the Father and the Spirit went to the cross. He endured it all without shirking any of it, he received directly the blows that were set upon him, and now all of that is finished. Shortly, there will be the long silence. The preacher, whose sermons challenged so many, will be ended.

That business between us and God, that unpleasantness begun in the Garden, that tendency to be gods unto ourselves, our rebellion, our clinch-fisted, violent pride, that sin, all that is about to be addressed, not with words, but with a deed. Jesus is about to do for us that which we cannot—have shown time and again we cannot—do for ourselves. We are about to learn that discipleship is not first a matter of our doing something for God but a matter of having something done for us by God.

How different is this God who decides, moves, acts, suffers, finishes, and accomplishes from the rather tame, flaccid, deistic deity that one hears about in much of contemporary mainline Protestantism! We've made up a god who creates a world in Genesis 1 and then retires. That's as much of a god as we can take.

The deistic god may be compassionate and caring, but never active. Listen to our prayers, which are mostly about us:

"Oh Lord, help us to see our responsibilities for making the world a better place. Set before us our duties and give us the strength to put the world aright."

We do not bother God with our petitions because we have become, in modernity, gods unto ourselves.

A friend pointed out to me that Mary's song in Luke 1, the so-called Magnificat is all in the past tense! Mary sings, "My soul magnifies the Lord. . . . he has looked. . . . the Mighty One has done. . . . he has scattered the proud. . . . He has brought down the powerful . . . and lifted up the lowly" (Luke 1:46-52).

So confident is Mary in the active work of her God, so robust is her faith in God's determination to do for us that which we could never do for ourselves, that she sings exclusively in the past tense!

"And I lay down my life for the sheep. . . . No one takes it from me, but I lay it down of my own accord. I have power to lay it down, and I have power to take it up again. I have received this command from my Father" (John 10:15-18).

Though his completing work is invisible to us—all we can see from here is the horror and the blood, the defeat and the death—though we look on his cross and see nothing but the last, the end, the loss, something grand and glorious is being worked out despite us. No need for you to be busy trying desperately to get yourself right with God. Sit there in the silence and just watch Jesus do as he dies. It is finished.

Earlier, back on the road, when he said, "I've got a baptism to be baptized with, and how I am constrained until it is accomplished" (AP). Well, back then, we didn't know what he was talking about. Now we know. He is talking about the accomplishment, the completion, the fulfillment of his work. He is talking about his death. Now, the baptism of his death is accomplished.

Jesus is presented in the Gospels as the most peripatetic, the most frenetic of teachers. He was always on the move, never alighting long in one place. A word here, a story there, then off to elsewhere. Now he is still, at rest.

How did he say "It is finished"? I think he said it not in defeat—I've done the best I could, now I give up, give in, and die—but in victory—I've fought the fight, faced Satan down, and now my work is stunningly accomplished. The scapegoat who took on the sins of Israel, driven out into the wilderness to die, has now become the Lamb of God who, driven back to the throne of God, atones for the sins of the whole world.

As Paul says, the only righteous One who knew no sin was made to bear all our sin that we sinners might become the righteous of God (1 Cor. 1:30). Don't ask me to explain that thick thought. You are not meant to figure it out, just sit there this day and behold it.

As we once said in the old Communion prayer, "he offered there for us a full, sufficient, and perfect sacrifice for the sins of the whole world." God has now finished the work that God began with us so long ago. God was determined, having created us, having loved us in so many and diverse ways, to get back to us. And now God has. It is finished.

Listen to this, oh ye purpose-driven, upwardly mobile, goal-setting high achievers. He has done what we could not do. Because we could not get up to God, God climbed down to us, got down on our level, and here, in the bloody, unjust crucifixion, we have at last descended to our level. God has finished what God began. It is finished.

What now is to be done by us? Nothing.

What might we learn from the lessons of this day? Nothing.

What are we supposed to do for God before nightfall? Nothing. Did you miss his words? "It is finished."

I recall C. S. Lewis's story, in *The Great Divorce*, in which the bishop (!) dies and finds himself getting off a bus in some unknown place. "Welcome to heaven," someone says to him. The bishop promptly presents himself to the person who seems to be in charge. "Where will we be gathering for the meeting?" he asks. (Bishops are addicted to meetings.) There is no meeting, he is told. "Well, there must be a meeting. There is work to be done, good to be accomplished, problems to be addressed. We are responsible people who have responsibilities. When is the meeting?"

No meeting. No work to be done. No responsibilities to be met. It's done. Over. Finished. God has done it all for us.

The story ends with the bishop boarding a bus bound for hell, eager to get there and get busy. Heaven is a place of blessed rest; hell is where the work is never done.

I confess that when I think of my church family, the Methodists, at worship, the image that pops up in my mind is that of a group of people who come to church with notepads in order to get our assignment for the week.

"This week, church, work on your racism, your sexism, and your manners. Come back next week, I'll give you another assignment," says the preacher.

No wonder we leave worship more depressed and burdened than when we arrived.

It's all about us. It's up to us to settle up the accounts between us and God or they won't be paid. It's all about us.

I read a sermon from a popular preacher entitled, "How To Get More Out of Worship." He gave about eight rules for how to make worship happen in your own soul. "You only get as much out of the service as you put into it," he advised.

Hardly a mention of anything God might do. It's all about us.

The Letter to the Hebrews tells of that great High Priest in the heavens who, when he had made the full, perfect, final sacrifice, sat down (Heb. 10:12). Most priests must be busy, doing good, trotting back and forth from the people to the altar, sacrificing, working, conducting three-hour services on Good Friday, getting ready for Easter, contributing to our relationship with God. But this Great High Priest, when he had done it all, says Hebrews, sat down. He sat down because it was finished. If the world only knew that the cross, that sign of humiliation and defeat, is God's greatest victory, the world would be reconciled to God. And we busy-bee sinners, so busy with our spiritual practices, our religious rites, our purpose-driven churches, our moral achievements (anybody who would come to a three-hour service, and on a Friday, has got to be good at being good!), and we in our busyness are forced this day to sit down, to be still and know that he is God, to be quiet, and simply to adore the wonder of his completed work in our behalf. This day we come to church planning to get on with the business of getting right with God only to be told by the church to do nothing but to be still, to sit, and to listen.

That business between us and God that began in the Garden, in which we first chose our wills over God's will, in which we rebelled and never looked back, this bloody business in which we, down through all the ages, always turned away from God, that is being fixed, finished this decisive day. So all you frenetic spiritual busybodies and anxious, purpose-driven do-gooders hear this: the sad dealings between us and God can only be finished by God. We've run up debts that can't be covered by us. The good news: the battle is done. The war is won. The debt is paid. It is finished.

Maybe, Lord Jesus, by praying this prayer, by reading this book, by paying really close attention to the sermon, by writing this down, we can get a grip on your sacrifice and our atonement. The strangeness of this day, the gore of what we have witnessed, the oddness of a crucified God, the incongruity of much that you have said in your Seven Words, well, it all tends toward a crisis of understanding. When we ask why, we expect an answer. And here at the end, we still haven't heard a really satisfying answer. And we cannot go home without answers.

We want to know so that we can better order our world, make sense out of this troubling mystery, then label it, box it up, render it in PowerPoint, and get on with our lives. For us, knowledge is control, and we so want to be in control.

After all, didn't you make us as sentient beings? You gave us the gift of conceptualization and the talent for figuring things out. We're not bragging, but don't you think we have done rather well with explaining just about everything? We've got a reliable epistemological method. We can uncover the keys to a really great church. We can ascertain the meaning of life. We can articulate the nine fundamentals of the Christian faith, the six purposes of a successful church, the three most important things to remember before we die. We can find a way to make marriage work. We can discover the short steps toward a better tomorrow. We can get a surefire way from here to there, a knock-down argument that will silence all interpretive conflict. We can, if we only believe that we can.

Thank you, Jesus, for allowing us to be born in an enlightened, progressive culture like Pasadena or Peoria where we know so much, so damned much. Amen.

Postprayer: Lord, on the other hand, once we think about it, if we could explain it, figure it out, get a grip on the cross, then we wouldn't need faith in you. Please, Lord, be more to us even than an explanation. Be our salvation. Deliver us from our lust for final elucidation. Save us from our best and worst selves; do that for us which we cannot, in our sin, do for ourselves. Go ahead and save us, no matter what you have to do. Amen.

The Seventh Word

"*Father, into thy hands I commend my spirit.*"
—Luke 23:46-49

It was a play that became a movie with William Hurt, *Whose Life Is This Anyway?* You know the answer to the play's question: "By God, my life is *mine!*" The irony is that the dying doctor who so raged against others taking charge of his life was doing so precisely in that time when we are dramatically confronted with the truth that our lives are definitely *not* and never have been our own: death. Death is the ultimate rip-off, the ultimate reminder that our vaunted boasts about self-possession are delusions. In one of his parables, Jesus compared God to a thief who comes in the night, while we are asleep and think we are secure, and steals everything we've got. Not the nicest image of God, to be sure, but a truthful one. In the end, God is going to rip off everything that we thought we had. In the end, the One who so graciously gave life is also the one who so unexpectedly takes it. Nobody has a right to take anything from anyone else without permission unless he owns what he takes in the first place.

Recently, at a conference on higher education, a speaker, speaking on the moral development of students, said that she thought the purpose of higher education was to foster the "art of self-possession by students." We possess cars, houses, why not also ourselves? I thought that an honest admission of the bankruptcy of much of American Higher Education. What we thought to be a four-year path toward wisdom is reduced to mere training in being more savvy consumers. You go to college to nurture the illusion that your life is your life to utilize as you please.

The church, at its best, has always known this to be a lie. Church is where we go to be reminded that the life we live is not our own. In the church in which I grew up, we were sometimes urged to "commit your life to Christ." There was a youth service, the preacher preached, then we all stood and sang, "Take my life, and let it be consecrated, Lord, to thee." In other words, we admitted, with this God, there is no decision to "commit your life to Christ." He doesn't accept your life as much as he takes it, since it's God's to begin with.

I made a call to a pastor whom I had just appointed to move to a church where the salary was seven thousand dollars less than the meager salary he was making at his present church. I called him to offer him condolence.

"Although I think this church is a good match with your gifts, the Cabinet and I do regret that we are having to ask you to take such a large cut in salary."

The pastor thanked me for my concern, then he said, "Bishop, I want you to tell the Cabinet not to worry. There is no way they can hurt me financially as bad as Jesus hurt me when he called me into this ministry. I was pulling down eighty-five thousand a year when Jesus grabbed me and made me go to seminary. Tell the Cabinet that there's nothing they can do to hurt me as bad as Jesus has already hurt me."

Like the prophets say, it is a fearful thing to fall into the hands of a living God.

Now, with this final word on Friday, Christ commits his life—and his death—to God.

We're at the end. And at the end, as he breathed his last, Jesus resumes the cruciform conversation that he began with his Father. He began with, "Father, forgive them." Now he ends with the crucial words, "Into thy hands I commend my spirit." Jesus does in his death what he did throughout his life, committed himself into the Father's keeping. Thus Christians believe that Jesus' death means as much as his life means. It wasn't simply that he died. It was the way he died. If he had died peacefully in his sleep, if someone had put a bullet through his head while he was trying to give a sermon, if his anguish alone had been the last word, his death would not mean what the church believes it means. At the end, in dying, the suffering Son committed himself to the receiving Father, giving the Father that which only the Son could give, which only the Father could receive.

When I was a college chaplain I spent a good deal of time with young adults pondering the persistent question, what will I do with my life?

This fateful Friday Jesus has got me to wondering, what will I do with my death? Most of us hope to die in such a way that we will die without knowing that we are actually dying. There was a day when people prayed that they would die with enough time to make peace with God and with the people whom they had wronged. Nowadays, most of us hope to die in such a way—a blow to the head, a skip of the heartbeat, an explosion in the brain—that we will go so quickly and painlessly that we will also go thoughtlessly, that is, that we will never know that this is it. *Finis.*

There was a time when people prayed that they would be given precious time at the end to call in their progeny and give them their last words of wisdom. Most of us hope for a quick death because, if we had the time to tell our children what we had learned from life, what on earth would we say? "Buy low, sell high"?

Jesus had three long hours to die, and he used his last moments well. He spoke to God, to a thief, to his family, his followers, and now, at the very end, again to his Father. "Into thy hands I commend my spirit."

The Bible says, "It is a fearful thing to fall into the hands of the living God" (Heb. 10:31 KJV). Presumably it is not a fearful thing to fall into the hands of a dead god. A dead god is otherwise known as an idol, a work of human spirituality and imagination, a "god" who is but our own sweet concoction (Flannery O'Connor). This no-god is not fearful at all since it is an idol that is created through our own wish projection to serve our selfish needs. But to have one's life grabbed, commandeered by a living God, that's a fearful thing.

It takes guts to give our most precious possession—our lives—over to God. (It takes guts to admit, at the end, when all is said and done, that it is a lie that our lives are our possessions to give. It takes grace to admit that our lives are God's gifts to take. Death tells the truth about that widespread deceit and conceit, which perhaps explains why we go to such extraordinary lengths, when we can afford it, to extend our lives through technology. However, death can't teach us anything unless we are given the grace, while living in a culture of deceit, to take the truth, and take it straight.)

It is a fearful thing to commend our spirits to God because, well, who knows what God will do with our lives? If you have commended your life to God on a Sunday morning, only to be shocked and dismayed by what God commanded you to do on a Monday morning, you know what I mean. Our only reassurance from God is the promise that God will never allow anything worse to happen to us than God allowed to happen to his only Son. There, does that make you feel better?

I think most of us, or maybe this is just me, but most of us spend most of our lives attempting to get our lives out of God's hands and into our own. We achieve, and work, and build and hoard, we work out at the gym and watch our cholesterol. For most of us, if God wants my life, then God will have to damn well come out and get it.

And truth to tell, by the end, one way or another, God does. We die.

Writer and preacher, Robert Farrar Capon, committed a great moral lapse that caused pain to himself and to those whom he loved. He committed adultery. When he confessed his infidelity to his wife, his life fell apart. He was nothing, lost, as good as dead. Capon says that it was there that he discovered that life in Christ comes through a kind of dying. Here is his account of how this event unfolded and what he learned the hard way:

> Almost from the start of my life as a priest, I was a pretty good preacher. . . . But I never quite got around to being a passionate enthusiast over what God had done for me personally in Jesus. Why? Well, I now think it was because I believed, back then, that I wasn't broken enough to need fixing. But some twenty years ago, after a long love affair (twenty-four years!) that was my marriage, I committed the unpardonable romantic sin of infidelity to the beloved, and made the monumentally stupid mistake of confessing it to the beloved herself—all in an unshakable assurance that I could repent so persuasively that she'd have to forgive me. (At the time, that was . . . my idea of repentance: a negotiation in which I was certain that my sincerity would give me the upper hand.)
>
> But it didn't. . . . My first reaction, of course, was denial: it just couldn't be happening. My second reaction, though, was

anger: She had to forgive me, damnit! (I won't even bother you with my other reactions. . . . One way or another, they were . . . attempts to get back what I thought of as my control over the situation—to get my life back to where I felt it belonged, namely, with me in the driver's seat.)

Then it slowly began to dawn on me that my control wasn't going to come back: I was going to have to face something I'd never seriously faced before: I was powerless. . . . My control hadn't slipped; it was gone. But in the end—and with me fighting the realization every inch of the way—the truth came to me: it wasn't that I was powerless, or out of control, . . . or hurt. I was dead. I had no more influence than a corpse over my own life.[1]

Capon got life, only through death. That seems to be a conventional path toward tradition.

When I was preparing to be a pastor, I took a quarter of Clinical Pastoral Education (CPE) in a hospital where I learned to care for the sick and the dying. I remember the day this man came in, forced by the staff to enter in a wheelchair, cursing and shouting at the staff all the way in. He brought his secretary with him for important business that no one could do but he. I was told not to attempt to visit him because he was a CEO who would be on the phone most of the day. Besides, he didn't care for clergy. I heard he was deathly ill but refused to accept the diagnosis and that he flew in a specialist from Minnesota! Each day I witnessed a stream of corporate underlings in and out of his room receiving their assignments. I tried to visit him and he cursed me, screaming that the hospital had better get his problem fixed and that he had no time to waste on little would-be CPE preacher boys.

How well I remember the afternoon that I heard loud wailing coming from his room. A nurse ran down the hall calling, "Get the chaplain, quick; Mr. Smith has finally got the truth and has had a breakdown."

"Well, perhaps I could help," I said.

"I need a real chaplain," said the nurse.

The older, wiser chaplain ambled down the hall, entered Mr. Smith's room. Things got very quiet. Finally the chaplain emerged and grumbled to me on his way back down the hall, "God got another one."

Oscar Wilde wrote about the redemption that comes only when we are in the depths of despair in his "Ballad of Reading Gaol" where he asks how in the world might a person's soul be cleansed of sin. "How else but through a broken heart / May Lord Christ enter in?"[2]

"I fled Him, down the nights and down the days; / I fled Him, down the arches of the years," says Francis Thompson, the poet of "Hound of Heaven." Some of you know firsthand what it's like to get pursued, stalked, tracked down by a living God. It's a fearful thing.

*Well, that's **not** what we are talking about now.*

We are talking about One so close, so one with the living God, that He could do what we, in our poverty, cannot, namely, to commend himself—the significance of what he had done, the purpose of his whole life and work, the darkness of death—hand all that over to God. A pursuing God did not have to pursue his only Son. In death, the Son pursued the Father, willingly, exuberantly commending his spirit to his Father who never stopped pursuing him. This word, this way of death, is as much a confirmation of the Son's oneness with the Father as the Son's divinely wrought birth.

In an earlier day, long ago, we Wesleyans once proudly pointed to the instances of "Happy Death," among us, those deaths in which the Christian, being so perfected in love, so close to God, slipped into death with a joy that comes from a short journey from life through death, to God. I fear that we have very few

"Happy Deaths" today because most of us, in death, make a very long and arduous trip from total self-absorption in this life to a most anguished and reluctant total self-loss in the next.

Jesus, on the other hand, had not a long way to go toward the Father, since He and the Father are One. Not long ago, an alleged theologian accused God the Father of "child abuse" in the death of Jesus, charging the Father with some sort of "sick" expiation of the sins of others through the violent sacrificial death of his only child. The sickness in this accusation is the overlooking of the fact that we are dealing with the Trinity here. God—Father, Son, and Holy Spirit—is One. When the Son suffers, presumably the Holy Spirit and Father are in anguish so that the whole Creation heaves. When the Son commends his life to the Father, presumably the Son is giving himself over to that which he truly is already. In commending himself to the Father, in his dying, the Son is dramatically demonstrating the unity of this divinity, the deep unity at the heart of the diverse Trinity.

One way you can tell a true God from a homemade idol is that idols tend to promise us continuity, immortality, and security, being mirrors of our ideal selves. Israel was forced to leave the security of a well-functioning economy in Egypt and live with the freedom that God pushed her into in the uncertain wilderness. Our lust for "security" causes us to have the largest military budget of any country in the world. We so hope to establish ourselves by ourselves, in certainty and security, through our military hardware, our pension systems, our burglar alarms. Israel learned that the major threat to her security was not the Canaanites but rather the Lord. The prophets had to tell her that all attempts at "security" tend to be efforts to establish ourselves by ourselves, that is, *idolatry*. But Israel existed only by God's act. "It was because the LORD loved you" (Deut. 7:7-8). Israel had no foundation, no means of existence, no secure reason for being here today or tomorrow, except as an undeserved, unearned, gracious act of God. Israel had to learn to worship her Lord even when circumstances (the exodus, the exile) did not warrant such confidence in God's creative love. Abraham, the father of the faith of Israel, had to venture out to he knew not where if he would walk with this God and be open to the promises of this God (Heb. 11:1). Only God knew where Abraham was being taken. Abraham and Sarah had to let go and let God lead. Of course the ultimate letting go, the ultimate exodus and the final exile, the greatest of all insecurity is the annihilation of death. So when Christians speak of cross and resurrection, we are saying something akin to what Israel said when she remembered exodus. We were nothing; then we were something, because of God. And we very well could be nothing again without God. Our only security is that much-evaded insecurity that is called fidelity to a living God or, as Jesus puts it here, "Father, into thy hands I commend my spirit."

Paul says that we, the baptized, are to live in such a way that, "united with him in a death like his, we will certainly be united with him in a resurrection like his" (Rom. 6:5). That's our hope. We have a choice, whether vainly to attempt to preserve ourselves by ourselves or instead to die like Jesus, commending ourselves and all those whom we love in death to the Lord, the Giver of Life. (Forgive me for thinking it sad that Christians, who ought to be just dying to commend ourselves to God, fight so valiantly and so expensively to commend those whom we love to the gods of technology, sucking oxygen and Medicare long after their apportioned lives have run their course, anything to avoid commending our spirits, and theirs, to God.)

So in commending his life to the Father, Jesus' last word is a take-charge, direct, strangely confident word. "Father, into thy hands I commend my spirit." For the last hours, Jesus has been arrested, bound, whipped, pulled to and fro from the Praetorium, then before the screaming crowd, humiliated, mocked, horribly violated. But now, at the end of this day in which he has been so used and abused, he takes charge, assumes command, unites with that One with whom he always was in unity. "Father, into thy hands I commend my spirit."

Do not hear these words as relenting, giving in, or giving up. Jesus is here commanding, commending, and committing, going head-to-head with the powers that be, decisively taking charge.

Earlier, from the cross, Jesus had quoted the psalm—"My God, my God, why hast thou forsaken me?"

That psalm (Psalm 22) is quite a contrast with the psalm that immediately follows it, Psalm 23. "The LORD is my shepherd; I shall not want. He maketh me to lie down in green pastures. . . . thy rod and thy staff they comfort me" (KJV). Psalm 23 is, in my experience, the psalm people most often quote at the end, at the end of their lives, or when they are at the end of their rope. It is a psalm of complete childlike, dependent trust in God. In the Twenty-third Psalm, God is the One who leads, guards, prepares, and protects. There is nothing for us to do but to walk and to let ourselves be led.

But here, at the end, the case is different. Jesus does not so much submit as he takes charge. For the past twelve hours or so, Jesus has been in the hands of sinful women and men. Now, he takes his life into his own hands and lays his life into the hands of his Father. This is the great act of submission that, at least in our cultural context, is the act of supremely countercultural defiance.

To address God Almighty as "Father" is what Jesus taught us to be bold to say. "Our Father, who art in heaven." This is an intimate, filial, and wonderfully defiant moment. And it is also a moment of strangely confident resolution.

Here is a man, who has nearly bled to death, nails through his hands that fix him to the wood of the cross, nails through his feet, hanging there, naked, barely able to gasp, probably suffocating slowly to death, hung up like a piece of meat. His ought to be the ultimate image of inaction and passive acquiescence.

And yet, it is precisely at this moment that Jesus takes charge. He takes his life out of the hands of his tormentors and places it confidently in the hands of his Father. He will not let his crucifiers have the last word or determine the significance of the cross.

It is not news that Jesus is dying. You must die and I must die. All humans die. And with Jesus—having said the words that he said and done the deeds that he did, well, you knew from the first that he would not die a natural death. You knew from the first that he would die at the hands of those whom he had offended. So his death is not a surprise.

It is *the way* that he died that makes this a stunning moment. It is not simply that he died in horrible agony upon the cross. This is the way the world treats its prophets and its saints, as Jesus noted on occasion.

What he teaches us in this, the last word from the cross is, *there is a way to do it.*

As a pastor, I have been privileged to enter that holy, inner sanctum, where someone comes when, having battled some terrible illness, having valiantly used all of the scientific and medical resources at our disposal, having attempted to put on a cheerful face, then, having wept, having raged at the caughtness of it all, finally grows calm, relents, and is at peace. Peace, at the last.

But their peace is rarely that of noble defeat. No, from what I've observed, theirs is more often peace like that of Jesus. Having given over their lives to diverse doctors, having obeyed solicitous family and friends who told them to rest, to eat, to sleep, to turn over in bed, to get up and walk, to submit to chemotherapy, to put a good face on a bad situation, now they at last take charge of their own lives. They give God the most precious gift that God has so graciously given to them. So, at the last, they take their lives, the lives that death thought it was taking from them, and they graciously give it in offering to the God who gave it to them. In so doing they make the highest act of stewardship.

There is a way to do it.

I was discussing with a friend the work of a distinguished scholar. This scholar had labored for over fifty years in a rather esoteric area of classical studies. When he died, at age eighty, my friend and I had occasion to reflect upon his work. I said, "I would think that his groundbreaking work will be of lasting significance. Quite an achievement."

My friend replied, as people sometimes do, "God only knows."

I thought it was one of those everyday, habitual comments, that at that moment had great significance. To be truthful, that is about all that can be said at the end of any of our lives. What does all of this mean? Will any of it endure? Have we counted for something? God only knows.

Oh, we build monuments, we endow chairs at the university, we have children, we carve our names and dates in granite over our graves, committing our lives to institutions, to corporations, to tombstones, to books, and to our children. In our better moments we know this to be an exercise in vanity. Only God knows what, ultimately, our lives may mean. Only God can make our lives ultimately mean more than we ourselves can make them mean. Therefore we do best to consider our lives as oblation.

In an interview, the gifted writer James Baldwin said that, when he began writing, one of the greatest obstacles that he had to overcome was to be put in the "victim box," that is, to be forced to write as the eternal African American victim of white racism. Baldwin had grown up in Harlem, and he had suffered from the evils of a racist society. He could have written exclusively about that for the rest of his life and would have had plenty to say. Yet he decided that to do so would have been to allow the world to define him essentially as a victim, and this he was unwilling to do.

Please note now that there is therefore little of the victim in these last moments of Jesus' earthly life. We live in a culture of victimization, as many have noted. On the one hand, it is good that we recognize that there is injustice and that that injustice horribly scars the lives of those who are the victims of injustice. But victimization, though it is right to name it, ought not to be something that forever names us. To be a perpetual victim is always to have your life named, claimed, and determined by the victimizer. It is to give the perpetrator of injustice power over who you are and what you mean.

"O Jesus, they have treated you terribly. Not only were you rejected, betrayed by your own disciples, but you were also horribly abused, beaten, flesh torn apart, limb ripped from limb and hung up in humiliating death. They so horribly took your life."

In one last, instructive word, Jesus teaches us:

No one took my life. I gave my life. I committed my life to my Father.

> He is the image of the invisible God, the firstborn of all creation; for in him all things in heaven and on earth were created, things visible and invisible. . . . He himself is before all things, and in him all things hold together. He is the head of the body, the church; he is the beginning, the firstborn from the dead. . . . For in him all the fullness of God was pleased to dwell, and through him God was pleased to reconcile to himself all things, whether on earth or in heaven, by making peace through the blood of his cross. (Col. 1:15-20)

At the end of the Good Friday service, we move into darkness, darkness and silence. So many words have been said this week.

We have performed so many dramatic liturgical activities. Now there is nothing left for us but silence and stillness. We have not in our devices the means to make all this work out. Here is a tragedy—the death of God's own Son—that we cannot fix. Only God knows what all of this shall mean. All the words that Jesus has spoken, all the deeds that Jesus has done, it is now up to God to make it all mean. The next move is up to God. Jesus has taken his life, all that he is, all that he has said and done and been, and given it over to the creative Father and the resourceful Spirit. In one last, confident, reckless act of faith, the Son has commended his spirit to the Father. The next move, the last move, as it always is, is God's. In the end, God. We shall see what all these Seven Words mean by the time we get to Sunday when God—Father, Son, and Holy Spirit—shall have the last word.

We will do ourselves an injustice, we will mess up the meaning of this story if we are not back here in church for Easter, the last word that is the first. It is vitally important to keep the Supper on Thursday, the Crucifixion on Friday, and the Resurrection on Sunday together, what the church called the *Triduum*, the "Three Days." The story sets up a need for a conclusion that only the Father can give. So in a way, we also are placing our fates into the hands of the Father, counting on the Father to end the story of the Son in which we have played our bloody roles but can never bring to a satisfying end.

One of the theological perils of focusing upon the death of Jesus on the cross is not only that we might forget the resurrection but also that we might overlook the Trinity. We must talk about the suffering of Jesus as the suffering of the Son, who willingly, obediently, in the power of the Holy Spirit, is sent by the Father for our salvation. The Son's suffering is a definition of who God the Father is and what the Holy Spirit does. Here, on the cross, "God was in Christ reconciling the world to himself" (2 Cor. 5:19, alt.

ending), and in resurrection the Son's sacrifice was vindicated as the act of a loving Father whose love extends, in the work of the Holy Spirit, to the whole sinful world. Jesus is no solitary individual of significance in himself. He's always completely about his Father's business (Luke 2:49), especially in this business on the cross. Wrestling with his Father's will at Gethsemane (Mark 14:16), or dying on Calvary, committing his life and his cause totally into the Father's hands (Luke 23:46), all this is in complete solidarity and in intimate relationship with his Father.

You can see the theological implications of saying that the One on the cross is trinitarian. Never again should any consider the cross as a mere moral example of how a good man got it in the end; it is a cosmic claim about who Almighty God is and what God does. It's a new definition of our word *almighty*. Never again should any lament that God is too grand, too big and ethereal to be known by mere mortals like us; God the Father reveals himself in the suffering of his Son. This God has a face and a way of being in the world with us. Never again should any assume that the Holy Spirit is a rather flaccid, vague, spiritual force; the Holy Spirit is the Spirit that proceeds from the Father, who was willing to sacrifice his only Son and the Son, who on the cross, was willing to offer himself totally to the work and will of the Father.

Just before he went to Jerusalem to die, Jesus told a story (Mark 12:1-12) about a Father who owned a vineyard. The vineyard was leased out to some tenants who treated it poorly and refused ever to pay rent. The Father sent his servants to collect on the rent that was his due, and the wicked tenants sent the servants packing, refusing to give the Father his rightful rent. Down through the centuries, the Father sent servant after servant, prophets who attempted to get the tenants to do right by the Father. Finally, in exasperation and with risk, the Father sent his only Son. Surely they will receive the Son as the emissary of the Father.

But the wicked tenants murdered the Son.

We just can't stand for there to be a Father. We are offended that all that we have, and all that we are, is on loan, a sacred trust from the Father. Therefore we despise the prophetic representatives of the Father and eventually we even kill the Son. All of which suggests that one of the most radical, offensive things Jesus commanded of us is, "When you pray, say, 'Our Father. . . .'"

Those of us who know a God who comes to us, is willing to be crucified by us, and who rose from the dead despite us can never be sure that we have in our power to be done with God. To what ludicrous depths of self-deprecation this God will go! After Bethlehem and Golgotha, we know that we shall never be safe from the invasions of this God. We shall never again be safe in our concepts, our questions, and our reasons. The Trinity intrudes precisely into those places where we wouldn't expect God to go.

And after the cross, God will never be safe from us. God has freely, willingly determined to be in solidarity with us, for us—perhaps the most risky decision God ever made. God comes to us in a form that allows us to reject him, to mock and ignore him. The merciful God places himself at our mercy. Surely God's greatest pain and suffering is not that of the cross but of our continual, daily, moment-by-moment betrayal. Love and death seem to go together, at least for the God who would dare bend toward us.

What will the Father do now that we have stooped to killing the only Son in a vain attempt to get God off our backs? As was so typical of his narrative style, Jesus does not finish this parable of the wicked tenants. Perhaps he could not finish the story because it was a story about the cross, a story that could only be ended by the Father, in one great, decisive setting things right as they could only be set right, by the Father. Now that we've done our worst, we tenants of the vineyard shall have to commend our fate into the hands of the Father. Jesus is now silent, without having ended the lesson. Here is a story so cosmic, so severe, so awful and tragic that only God knows how to end it. How long will we have to wait for the Father to end the story, in the Father's own way?

At least three days.

But for now, on this day, we've heard Jesus' last word. Pray to God that you might have the grace, and the faith too, to make it your last word, your final prayer, "Father, into thy hands I commend my spirit."

Notes

1. Robert Farrar Capon, *The Foolishness of Preaching: Proclaiming the Gospel against the Wisdom of the World* (Grand Rapids: Eerdmans, 1998), 26-27.

2. Oscar Wilde, "The Ballad of Reading Gaol," written in Paris, 1897; published 1898.

Afterword

Christians keep forgetting how odd it is to be a Christian nowadays, or any other. It might be possible for us to think that the Christian faith makes sense, that it is a helpful means of making our lives more purposeful, another technique for making us a bit less miserable. But then comes Good Friday, when the church makes us stare for three long hours and contemplate the cross. And it's then that we know how very odd it is for God Almighty not to turn away from killers like us and for us not to turn away from a crucified Savior.

Just for now, let's do something a little odd for the North American church. Let's define a "Christian" as that person who really believes that Good Friday is more important in the scheme of things than Mother's Day.

When I was a college chaplain, a group of students approached me to ask for my help. They wanted a corner of the Duke Gardens to be designated as a "Spiritual Center."

"What's a 'Spiritual Center'?" I asked.

"It's a place in the garden, perhaps with a comfortable bench, where we could go and meditate. A quiet place, secluded by trees or shrubs, preferably. All natural."

"What would you do there?" I asked.

"Nothing," they replied, "except to just sit quietly and meditate."

"Meditate on what?" I asked.

"Just meditate. Think about nature, or ourselves, God or whatever," they answered.

I realized then and there how odd it is to be a Christian. I told the students that, though I hated to disappoint them, I couldn't muster any enthusiasm for their "Spiritual Center." I was a Christian, we're not at all "spiritual," if by spiritual one means sitting quietly and staring either at ourselves or a shrub. We're not spiritual. We are incarnational. We like flesh to look at when we're attempting to look at God. And the flesh we look at is bleeding and has some nasty holes through it, nothing natural about it. The great theologian, Karl Barth, says that a preacher has nothing better to do than to stand like John the Baptist and, with a boney hand, point people toward the cross.[1] On this Friday, we pay attention to that which the world has a myriad of ways of passing by.

I don't expect today's spiritual voyeurs to understand what I'm talking about, for this way of thinking is against just about everything we contemporary North Americans think about God. We are conditioned to think that we get to God by first delving more deeply into ourselves whereas the cross says that God gets to us by forcing us to focus upon something other than ourselves.

Added to the liability of our narcissism, when we encounter suffering or pain, we are conditioned to turn away. We don't have public hangings anymore and we think that's a sign of humanitarian progress. We execute our convicted murderers in private, safe from the prying public gaze. We think it's OK for the state to kill people, as long as no one actually sees the state killing anyone. Remember how much trouble the photographer got into during the aftermath of the Iraq war for having the bad taste to publish a photo of flag-draped coffins of U.S. soldiers?

I suspect that our turning away from suffering and pain has less to do with the progress of our humanity and everything to do with our lacking the spiritual or intellectual resources to confront the massive amount of suffering and pain that afflicts human life. We have nothing to do with our suffering other than to take a pill or to turn away.

When Hurricane Katrina devastated the South, the media got us worked up, for a while. Then we moved on to other news. Some commentator said of Katrina, "that we are so shocked and appalled by this storm is an indication of how little we know or care about the mass of humanity and its suffering. Homelessness, lack of food and water, is how millions live every day. Deal with it." Well, that's just the problem, isn't it? We have few theological resources for dealing with undeniable tragedy and vast human pain, so we develop our means for looking in the other direction.

What I'm saying is that staring at an innocent man suffocating and bleeding to death on a cross is not our idea of a fine way to spend three hours on a Friday.

Yet in looking at the cross of Christ we are looking at considerably more even than excruciating (no pun intended) human pain. Christians believe that when we look at Jesus on the cross and meditate on that meaning, we are privileged to see as much of God as we ever hope to see. The cross is not simply the truth about the human condition; it's the truth about God. Of all the things that might be said about us and God, the cross is the most crucial (no pun intended). The cross is not simply a ghastly sight of a naked man dying in agony, but also a full frontal disclosure of what God is up to in the world, a dramatic unveiling of who God really is, down deep. The cross is the crux of the matter between us and God (no pun intended). We really ought to call this Friday, Holy Friday, as the church has historically named this day, rather than Good Friday, for the goodness in this Friday requires considerable nuance to say just why Christians call the crucifixion of Jesus "good."

With the exception of Mel Gibson's pornographically gory *Passion of The Christ*, if we think about Jesus on the cross, we usually do so with suffocating sentimentality. About the most we mainline Christians can muster is that Jesus "identifies with us in our suffering," or on the cross, "Jesus is in solidarity with us." In other words, the best thing about Jesus is that he recognizes that my pain is more important than his. This misery-loves-company theology is immensely popular in a world where religion has become therapy and theology is sentimentality and religion is no good if it does not relieve some of my pain.

Well, there is nothing sentimental about a cross. As Luther says repeatedly, a theologian of the cross calls things by their real names. The cross becomes a lens through which everything is examined, the mirror in which reality is seen, the window into the facts of life. While it is true that in Christ God enters into our suffering and death, the suffering of Christ occurs not simply because Jesus has this thing for folk in pain but rather because we are at war with God, because we all want to be God, to put ourselves and our way up above God and God's way so we just naturally had to nail God's Son on a cross. We are the crucifiers more than the crucified. When we saw God-in-the-flesh Jesus, we didn't identify with him or feel grateful for his solidarity with us. Our words were an almost unanimous, "Crucify him!" His pain was not only from the nails but from the betrayal by his own disciples who forsook him and fled.

The cross renders us active, resourceful, gods-creating people into passive bystanders. Did you know that the word *passive* comes from the same root as *passion*, which in Latin means "to suffer"? It is not simply that Jesus stands beside us, strengthening us against the disappointment, the disease, and the death that makes us suffer. Rather, it is that in Jesus we passively suffer the strange work of a sovereign God. Even as Jesus endured his passion, so we are brought down low as he was brought low in Gethsemane. We too easily forget that God is not only compassionate but also holy, until we see God on the cross. In the cross we become victims, not of some sinister evil outside ourselves, some violent storm or earthquake, or even of that all-too-human evil within ourselves. We become victims of the workings of a sovereign and righteous God. The cross, as mirror of us, reveals not only that God is with us but that God is decisively against us. The cross is our most severe judgment, our grandest mercy. God cannot get to us as the world is, as we are, so a reaching, resourceful Trinity makes war upon us and our world through the suffering, sacrificial love of the cross and thereby changes everything.

To merely sentimentalize the cross, to enlist it in our culture of victimization, we hope to renovate ourselves from being crucifying sinners into suffering victims. And we so love to think of ourselves as victims. The cross is thereby therapeutically transformed into a bad thing that sometimes happens to good people rather than the ultimately good thing of God's "No!" to our presumed goodness. So in thesis 21 of the *Heidelberg Disputation*, Luther says that the "theologian of the cross" is determined to call things by their proper names. A "theologian of glory" calls "the bad good and the good bad." So the cross tells the truth about us.

The cross unmasks the perverse nature of our sin. Our sin is not in our acquiescence to our worst inclinations but rather in our pursuit of our best. It's not only that we do bad, which we do, but rather our worst is in our feverish attempts to take matters in hand and do well. This is what Luther means by a "theology of glory." Glory theology says that we are destined for onward and upward spiritual mobility. We can, if we only think we can, make progress, do better, and work good. This is New Age Religion all over, along with the popular and marketable spiritualities of this and that. Within us there is a divine spark, a ladder by which we can, if we only have faith that we can, through our earnest efforts, climb up to God. Progressive Christianity! We may die, but that divine, inner essence is eternal. Religion becomes just another technique to move us onward and upward and all that.

Paul says in Galatians 2:19-20 "I have been crucified with Christ; and it is no longer I who live, but it is Christ who lives in me. And the life I now live in the flesh I live by faith in the Son of God, who loved me and gave himself for me." By saying, "I have been crucified" Paul does not mean that he is going through a rough time just now. Rather, Paul points toward a mystery. Just as Jesus was crucified, brought low, humiliated, and made powerless by the cross, so are we. If we would follow Jesus, we've got to follow him through to the cross, our cross, the one he lays on our backs because we're following him. The cross subsumes us into that story. In Jesus, the cross becomes our story. Thus Luther could say, "the cross *alone* is our theology." As Luther said in one of his writings on the cross, "The real and true work of Christ's Passion is to make man conformable to Christ, so that man's conscience is tormented by his sins in like measure as Christ was pitiably tormented in body and soul by our sins."[2]

Too much contemporary worship is a form of consumerism—the gospel as another technique to enable us to feel a bit less miserable about ourselves by getting us even more deeply into ourselves. In our insufferably upbeat, incurably optimistic, mother-I-would-rather-do-it-myself economy, I'll be the first to admit that the cross story doesn't sell that well. It's the glory story that sells, for it comes quite naturally to us. The glory story Gerhard Forde calls "ladder theology"—theology as a means of climbing up to God. The glory story leaves us in control. Onward and upward.

The cross assaults glory theology in all its forms, emptying us, reminding us that we are dust. We live and learn by dying and being damned. As Paul says, the cross "destroys the wisdom of the wise." On Good Friday our stories of onward and upward become the more truthful tale of "ashes to ashes, dust to dust." Barbara Brown Taylor remembers a retreat where the leader asked people to think of someone who represented Christ in their lives. "When it came time to share our answers, one woman stood up and said, 'I had to think hard about that one. I kept thinking, "Who is it who told me the truth about myself so clearly that I wanted to kill him for it?"' "

"According to John, Jesus died because he told the truth to everyone he met. He *was* the truth, a perfect mirror in which people saw themselves in God's own light."[3] And the light was so truthfully bright and searing, so full of love that put the lie to all our thoughts about love, that we murdered him in a vain attempt to put out the light.

Perhaps that's why the church forces us to sit here, for a long time in the darkness, in the silence, listening to these seven words, staring at this thing before us, compelling us to talk about matters we would as soon avoid, stripping us of pretense and sham, revealing who we are even as we see who Jesus is. Jimmy Breslin said, "Only a fool would tell tales of his personal life, under any circumstances. A wife, consumed by guilt after a week with a boyfriend while her husband was away, sits at the kitchen table as he returns from his trip. She says grimly, 'We have to talk.' He slumps into a chair and sighs: 'You've found out about me!' "[4]

So let us not be surprised by the flood of truth-telling and candor that is evoked while staring at the cross. Only a fool would bare all for three hours on a Friday afternoon, only fools for Christ's sake.

And then on Easter, God vindicates the crucified Jesus through the resurrection, thus demonstrating whose side God is on and how God achieves God's victories. Because we couldn't climb up to God, God got to us, got down on our level, so to speak. It's a hard way to walk but Christians believe there is no other way to or from God. Thus Christians are able to speak in one breath both of the cross as God's great "No!" to human aspirations and deceit and also as God's great "Yes!" keeping cross and resurrection together.

"I'm going to lick this demon," said the newly reformed alcoholic. I wished him well. But I wasn't surprised to learn that, three months later, he was back in the depths of addiction. Eventually he "hit bottom," as they say, lost everything, in utter misery. It was then that he said, "I can't lick this thing by myself. I don't have it within me to quit drinking." And it was there that he began his upward ascent. Ironically, as long as he thought he had it in his power to save himself, he was doomed. When he knew, really knew, that he was doomed to know nothing about how to help himself, that he was powerless before a ten-dollar bottle of booze, then he was empowered by a force greater than himself. That's a cross sort of experience.

The theology of glory says that all we need is a whiff of inspiration, that the church is here to give us a bit of a boost, a bit of encouragement, to discover and to develop our better natures, to help us be more spiritual and morally fit. Autosalvation is the goal of all such ecclesiology. What seems at first glance to be good news—you can save yourself by yourself if you will only believe this, attend this church, feel this emotion, follow this spiritual discipline—eventually becomes the back-breaking bad news of constant, grueling, ultimately futile work. Little wonder that many of our very best church people—morally and spiritually speaking—seem so often exhausted. Whoever would make spirituality into a therapeutic system, a means of spiritual upward mobility, is in for a full-time job. If there really were a set of purposeful principles (sorry Rick Warren) through which we could get our lives together, then Jesus' death on the cross is the greatest mistake God ever made. Jesus should have explained the program to us, given us the appropriate technique, rather than died for us. Fortunately, Jesus knows that we're just not that effective in saving ourselves by ourselves.

A theology of the cross assumes, on the other hand, that a walk with Jesus tends to involve some sort of Via Dolorosa, a "hitting bottom," as recovering alcoholics say. We've got, on our own, no cure for what ails us. Sin has got us. Even our most noble and very best works are the results of our sin, as the cross of Jesus exposes. Jesus was nailed upon the cross for the very "best" of our reasons, our very "best" of ideals—biblical fidelity, law and order, respect for the authorities, religious commitment, and all the rest.

So everyone must learn to stand up and say, "My name is Will and I am a sinner," and the cross is the only means to get there.

When we focus on Good Friday in a book like this, when we speak of the cross in this tone of voice, we must always attempt to believe in cross and resurrection together. The very first followers of Jesus saw the significance of this dark Friday only in the light of Easter Sunday. On Easter, it wasn't that God resurrected the dead in general, rather, God resurrected the *dead Jesus*. Easter doesn't first of all mean that "we will see our loved ones when we die" but that when we look at the cross of Christ, we see the true nature of the triune God. When Jesus had said in John's Gospel, "I am the way, and the truth, and the life. No one comes to the Father except through me," he meant the truth that *this* way, this cruciform, Spirit-induced way is the only way to life in the Father. In the resurrection, God vindicated Jesus' way as the way. And what is that way? It is the way of the cross and resurrection.

> "Jesus of Nazareth, a man attested to you by God with mighty works and wonders and signs that God did through him in your midst, as you yourselves know—this Jesus, delivered up according to the definite plan and foreknowledge of God, you crucified and killed by the hands of lawless men. God raised him up." (Acts 2:22-24 ESV)

We had in mind a savior who would come to us with a plan for our saving ourselves by ourselves, a savior who could fix all that we thought wrong with the world. "But God. . . ." We begged for a savior who could get us out of our predicament with six easy steps toward a more purposeful existence. "But God" had Another in mind. The One whom God vindicated by raising him from the dead, this is the way of God, this One *is* God. To say "Jesus is risen" is to say "This is what God really looks like, this is who God is and whose side God is on." Try saying "God raised torturer Hitler from the dead" and see how far it gets you. Not too inspiring. To say "But God raised tortured Jesus from the dead" is to be let in on an open secret: this is what God is up to in the world. So whenever Christians say "God," we mean whoever put one over on the world by raising Jesus from the dead.[5]

Without the resurrection connected to the cross, Easter linked to Good Friday, we might be tempted to say that the way of the cross was a helpful technique for getting back toward God, a temporary setback that Jesus eventually overcame through his resurrection. We would have to say that the religious way is a demanding, difficult way, but it is a way that eventually, in the end, leads to a great heavenly reward that makes all the sacrifices worthwhile. There would then be room for heroic human sacrifice and sincere striving, hard work, and moral achievement. We could attempt to reconstruct the "historical Jesus" and try to live with whatever remains we dug up, going on believing anything about God that we found to be uplifting and psychologically useful. But the cross was utter annihilation, complete abandonment, forlorn death, real nothingness, destruction of all our collective attempts to say who God is and what God wants.

And yet, the resurrection is the grand testimony, not that the cross is a temporary setback but rather that this is the way of God with the world. It is of the nature of this God to win God's victories through suffering love. There is no other way for God to get to people like us without suffering our blood and injustice. And there is no other way for people like us to get to this God other than the way this God ordains, through death and resurrection, life from death, death as a way to life. In the face of the horror of the cross, only God can redeem such bleakness and defeat. And God redeems defeat through a stunning and surprising act of resurrection of the crucified, or there is no hope.

Without the resurrection, we are unable to tell the truth, which is the cross. There is a sense in which we could not stare at the cross all day on Good Friday were it not for our confidence in Easter. Nobody can possibly understand what we are doing in the liturgy of Holy Friday who isn't here for Easter Sunday. Of course, nobody can participate in the worship on Easter Sunday who wasn't here for three hours on Good Friday. Not that Easter negates the cross, rather it intensifies it, showing us the startling truth of a God who, for love of us, is willing to act not at all like a God ought to act.

Yet there can't be resurrection without death. In 1518, Luther was asked to defend his "New Theology" before his Augustinian brethren at Heidelberg. *The Heidelberg Disputation* is Luther's defense, a defense that he bases upon the truth of the cross. Luther had been attacking the notion of church-ordained spiritual disciplines and Christian practices (good works) as the way to God. The only way to God is the way from God—the cross. In the cross all of our presumed wisdom, strength, good works, and glory are shown to be the sham that they are, said Luther. This theologian of the cross tells the truth about God:

> This is clear: He who does not know Christ does not know God hidden in suffering. Therefore he prefers works to suffering, glory to the cross, strength to weakness, wisdom to folly, and, in general, good to evil. These are the people whom the Apostle calls "enemies of the cross of Christ" [Phil. 3:18], for they hate the cross and suffering and love works and the glory of works. Thus they call the good of the cross evil and the evil of a deed good. God can be found only in suffering and the cross, as has already been said. Therefore the friends of the cross say that the cross is good and works are evil, for through the cross works are dethroned and the Old Adam, who is especially edified by works, is crucified. It is impossible for a person not to be puffed by his good works unless he has first been deflated and destroyed by suffering and evil until he knows that he is worthless and that his works are not his but God's.[6]

For us, the cross is the infliction of deep suffering, the deep suffering that is caused when we realize the inadequacy of even our best works and our grandest ideas. On the cross, all that, including our vaunted spiritual aspirations, is condemned to death (1 Cor. 1:18-25). As Luther said, "When we were right, God laughed at us in our rightness." A theologian of glory sees suffering as unmitigatingly bad, something to be overcome, drugged, or explained away. A theologian of the cross sees suffering as a key to what is going on in the world, the central clue to our real condition and what God intends to do about it.

As you see in these meditations upon the Seven Words of the Cross, we've made a big deal out of just a few small words. Luther said that a person ought to not be allowed to preach until that would-be preacher was able to preach on just one word out of the Bible. Surely he was thinking of words like these seven. It is almost impossible for us to make too much of these particular words on this particular day.

Although the Christian celebration of a service on Good Friday, with recollection of the words and actions of Jesus on the cross, goes all the way back to the first centuries of the faith (Egeria, the fourth-century pilgrim nun, gives a detailed description of the service in Jerusalem on Good Friday), the Seven Words from the Cross is a relative late comer to Christian worship. The contemporary practice of a three-hour service focused upon the "seven last words of Christ," with sermonic meditations on each word or phrase, was probably invented by a seventeenth-century priest (Alonso Messia Bedoya, 1665–1732) in Peru. Some think that the service became popular in great part because of the trauma inflicted upon the area by a series of earthquakes that rattled Peru in 1687. Celebrating the Seven Last Words service in a church in the middle of Manhattan, shortly after the trauma that shook our nation on September 11, I found that these words had new resonance for those gathered there. Here are words that were spoken in the greatest shaking that the earth has known: the crucifixion of Jesus the Christ.

Normally, we don't have corporate worship on a Friday. Christians, at some very early date, ceased honoring the Sabbath and keeping it holy, even though the Torah demanded it. We began worshiping on Sunday, which we called "The Lord's Day." And because we have witnessed the joy and the triumph of the resurrection, as we celebrate it on Sunday, feasting at the Lord's Table in our churches, we are able, one day during the year, to worship on Friday from noon until three in the afternoon. This day we fast, we forswear our usual Sunday festive vestments, we sit in a darkened church, and we ponder nothing but words. The God who loved us enough to die for us, now loves us enough to speak to us, to teach one last lesson before dying, so that we, hearing and overhearing these words, might not only live forever but also learn forever to live with Him.

See how much pain it caused God to get close to us? We tend to kill our saviors and murder our messiahs. A God like the Trinity couldn't be close to people like us without a cross. The Trinity is perfect, ever-reaching total love and, as everyone knows, the conventional human response to relentless love is defensive, self-protective hate. And we can't be forever with this triune God without hearing this Friday a somber sermon that makes sense only in light of the joy of Sunday.

When one considers the frustrations that we have had, down through the millennia, in reaching up and out to God—the death-dealing delusions of our attempts to be gods unto ourselves, along with our simple, though intransigent ignorance of what God wants out of us—well, that's why we look upon a bloody cross and call it "good," that's why we say in unison, thank God it's Friday.

Notes

1. I have a great deal to say about that in my *Conversations with Barth on Preaching* (Nashville: Abingdon, 2006).

2. *Luther's Works* (ed. Jaroslav Pelikan and Helmut T. Lehmann; Philadelphia: Fortress Press, 1958–72), 42.7-14. Quoted by Gerhard O. Forde, *On Being a Theologian of the Cross: Reflections on Luther's Heidelberg Disputation, 1518* (Grand Rapids: Eerdmans, 1997), 7. I have been greatly helped by Forde in my thinking about a theology of the cross.

3. Barbara Brown Taylor, "The Perfect Mirror," *The Christian Century* 115, no. 9 (March 18-25, 1998): 283.

4. Jimmy Breslin, "You Can't Eat Honor," *Esquire* (October 1993): 176.

5. This colorful way of putting the matter is Robert W. Jenson's in his *Systematic Theology* (vol. 1; New York: Oxford University Press, 1997), 12, 31.

6. *Luther's Works*, 31.53. Quoted in Forde, *On Being a Theologian*, 82.

Index of Names

Index of Scripture